AELIUS ARISTIDES
AND
THE NEW TESTAMENT

STUDIA AD
CORPUS HELLENISTICUM
NOVI TESTAMENTI

EDIDERUNT

H. D. BETZ • G. DELLING

G. MUSSIES • W. C. VAN UNNIK †

VOLUMEN SEXTUM

P. W. VAN DER HORST

AELIUS ARISTIDES
AND
THE NEW TESTAMENT

LEIDEN

E. J. BRILL

1980

AELIUS ARISTIDES AND THE NEW TESTAMENT

BY

P. W. VAN DER HORST

LEIDEN
E. J. BRILL
1980

Published with financial support from the Netherlands Organization for the Advancement of Pure Research (Z.W.O.)

ISBN 90 04 06054 5

PRINTED IN THE NETHERLANDS

TABLE OF CONTENTS

PREFACE

In the series Studia ad Corpus Hellenisticum Novi Testamenti, four volumes have been published. Each volume has a very different mode of presentation. G. Petzke, in his book *Die Traditionen über Apollonius von Tyana und das Neue Testament* (1970), first gives a survey of the *traditionsgeschichtliche* and *formgeschichtliche* parallels between the writings and traditions on Apollonius, on the one hand, and, on the other hand, the N.T., especially the Gospels. Then he gives a survey of the *religionsgeschichtliche* parallels between life, works and words, of Apollonius and the N.T., especially the life, works and words, of Jesus. The main emphasis lies on the comparison of the historical Apollonius and Jesus, and the traditions about them. A quite different plan is found in G. Mussies' *Dio Chrysostom and the New Testament* (1972). Here we find a *seriatim* presentation of all kinds of parallels from Dio Chrysostom to passages from the N.T. So the book starts with parallels to Matt. I and ends with parallels to Apoc. XXII. Both the (Greek) text of the relevant passages from the N.T. and the text of the parallels from Dio Chrysostom are always fully quoted, though mostly without commentary, just as in the old Wettstein. Again, a wholly different plan is found in the third and fourth volumes by a team of American scholars, directed by H.-D. Betz, *Plutarch's Theological Writings and Early Christian Literature* (1975) and *Plutarch's Ethical Writings and Early Christian Literature* (1978). Here the text of Plutarch is taken as a starting-point. That is to say, from every treatise those passages are pointed out (in the order of Plutarch's text) to which parallels from the N.T. and other early Christian literature (from the second century) can be found. Neither the passages from Plutarch nor those from the Christian authors are quoted fully, but the parallels are provided with succinct comments.

Each one of these three methods has its own advantages and disadvantages. Petzke's method results in the most readable book; it is a continuous text about Apollonius' life and works, with constant reference to comparable phenomena in the N.T. The reader is not irritated by an excess of untranslated Greek. This approach however, makes it impossible to adopt materials from the traditions about Apollonius that are not important from the point of view of *Traditions-*, *Form-* and *Religionsgeschichte*. E.g. stylistic and grammatical parallels fall outside the scope of this book. Mussies' book is the most conveniently arranged: without effort the reader can find the required materials, and neither an edition of the N.T. nor one of Dio Chrysostom is needed in order either to read or, rather, to use this book. Everything can be found in the book itself, according to the method of Wettstein and other authors of *Observationes*. But its use will probably be restricted because of the great amount of Greek (the book consists for 90% in Greek quotations). The approach of Betz has the advantage that the reader is enabled to study the parallels in the framework of the treatises from which they come, so that they do not appear out of context. This method, too, ensures that parallels of all kinds can be indicated (as is the case with Mussies). But in order to consult the book, the reader must have both a text of Plutarch and of the N.T. as well as other early Christian writers to hand; otherwise it cannot be followed. Moreover, the accumulation of abbreviations and references makes hard reading. And this is more a collection of parallels from early Christian literature to Plutarch than from Plutarch to the Christian authors.

In view of the advantages and disadvantages of each of these three approaches, it was difficult in this case to find a method of presenting the materials. With some hesitation, a method has been chosen which closely resembles the one used by Mussies. The reasons for this are as follows. The materials worked through, i.e. 57 orations, do not offer the possibility of following the descriptive approach of Petzke. Moreover, if this method could have been used in this case, many of the parallels which have been incorporated in the text could not have been adopted. The method of Betz has not been followed because it cannot reasonably be expected that every N.T. scholar has an edition of the complete works of Aristides in his own library. For the sake of surveyability I have chosen the traditional *seriatim* presentation, in which the passages from Aristides are always quoted in full. But, unlike Mussies, the Greek text of the N.T. is quoted only if it was necessary to make clear to which part or which motif of the verse concerned the passage from Aristides is a parallel. This has the additional advantage that the book contains less Greek and becomes less voluminous.

I fully realize that the result of this method of listing parallels can be a serious misuse of the materials presented. Attention is only drawn to points where there seems to be a certain agreement or similarity, whereas it may rather be the absence of parallels that is very significant. The reader should continually keep this in mind and protect himself against over-estimating the parallel materials. The evaluation of these materials should be left open until more work in this field has been done and one can better identify those passages and concepts in the N.T. for which no parallels are to be found. Bearing in mind that only a small area has yet been studied in this way, it will not be surprising to find that in the long run a number of the parallels adduced by me turn out to be no parallels at all or to have little bearing upon problems of N.T. interpretation.

Utrecht
December 1978

P. W. van der Horst

[The fifth volume in this series, W. C. Grese's *Corpus Hermeticum XIII and Early Christian Literature*, Leiden 1979, was published too late to be included in the discussion in this Preface.]

INTRODUCTION

Life and works of Aristides

Publius Aelius Aristides lived from A.D. 117 till 180.[1] He was born at Hadriani in Mysia in a wealthy family, who were citizens of Smyrna and who received Roman citizenship in A.D. 123. His father was a priest of Zeus there. Aristides received the best rhetorical training available by studying with the greatest sophists of his day, in Smyrna, Pergamum, and Athens.

After he had decided to become an orator, he fell ill during a tour through Egypt in A.D. 142. This was the beginning of a life-long history of suffering and illnesses. He turned to the god Sarapis for improvement in his health, without much success. About December of 144, when he had almost given up his hope of becoming a successful orator (he had serious respiratory problems), he received his first revelation from Asclepius, the most important healing god of antiquity. His devotion to this god increased during his life, although Sarapis, Isis, Zeus, Apollo, Athena, and other gods retained their places in his eclectic polytheism.

From 145 till 147 he spent two years convalescing as a resident in the famous temple of Asclepius in Pergamum. The dreams and revelations he received from the god during this period of incubation contained many prescriptions for curing his illnesses, e.g. blood-letting, vomiting, diets, swimming in fast-flowing rivers during the winter, etc. He wrote an account of this and subsequent periods when he received revelations from his favourite god, the so-called Sacred Tales, Ἱεροὶ λόγοι, in which about 130 dreams have been preserved. These are highly interesting from a psychopathological point of view. As Behr says, they offer "a unique opportunity to analyse to some degree the psychology of at least one individual of the ancient world." [2] Among the other people at the temple were several well-to-do and high-ranking Greeks and Romans, "a

[1] This short account is based upon C. A. Behr's excellent monograph *Aelius Aristides and the Sacred Tales*, Amsterdam 1968. For details the reader is referred to that work.

[2] C. A. Behr, *Aristides* I (Loeb Classical Library), London—Cambridge (Mass.) 1973, X. See in the bibliography the publications by M. and D. Gourevitch, C. A. Meier, G. Michenaud and J. Dierkens.

small, cultivated circle of neurasthenics",[3] with whom Aristides spent much of his time.

In 147 he tried to become active again as an orator, convinced that not only his improved health, but also his rhetorical ability and career were due to Asclepius' grace. Oratory had become something sacred for him because of this fusion of religion and rhetoric. Aristides had to fight several battles in order not to be elected for civic offices in his country. He vehemently insisted upon his right to immunity because he felt too insecure to commit himself to any obligation. After 153 he began to travel a great deal (to Greece and Rome), and he now accepted students. These were his glorious years as an orator. However, in 165 smallpox spread throughout the empire, and Aristides fell ill. He recovered slowly, but fell ill again. According to his diary he dreamt in this period of crowded public declamations and he received all kinds of curious prescriptions for recuperation from Asclepius. The after-effects of these two serious illnesses in quick succession stamped the last fifteen years of his life. He still made public appearances, but his physical ailments and his religious fixation resumed. The earthquake by which Smyrna was destroyed in 177 marked the end of Aristides' career. Although he played an important role in the speedy reconstruction of the city by writing appeals to Marcus Aurelius and speeches to the governor and the citizens, he never again left his estates, where he died at the age of sixty-three. "All should agree that there was much sadness in his life." [4]

Although the great Reiske called him by far the most difficult Greek author after Thucydides,[5] Aristides was highly valued in antiquity for his precision of style and his high standards of Atticism. For many later orators and writers on composition he served as a model, until far into Byzantine times. This explains the great number of manuscripts of the works of Aristides; Behr lists 234 mss. and says he is certain the list is incomplete.[6] Many of Aristides'

[3] Behr, *ibid.*

[4] Behr, *Aelius Aristides and the Sacred Tales*, 115.

[5] This judgement of J. J. Reiske (from the Preface of his *Animadversiones in Graecos Auctores* III, Leipzig 1761) is reprinted in vol. III of Dindorf's edition of Aristides, p. 788.

[6] See the lengthy Introduction to vol. I of the great critical edition of Aristides by Behr (Leiden 1976). Here Behr not only discusses the extremely complicated manuscript situation, but he also gives a succinct but useful survey of the study of Aristides from the end of the Byzantine period up to the present day.

writings have been lost. Of the fifty-seven extant works printed in the Dindorf edition, six are certainly spurious: both treatises *Ars Rhetorica* A and B; [7] ors. 53 and 54 Dind.; [8] and ors. 9 Dind. (= 35 Keil) and 43 Dind. (= 25 Keil). The fifty-one authentic works are classified by Behr [9] as follows: 1. treatises (e.g. the writings against Plato); 2. panegyrics and symbouleutic speeches to cities or on public questions; 3. speeches on rhetoric; 4. speeches to individuals and funeral orations; 5. declamations; 6. religious speeches and writings (the hymns to the gods and the Sacred Tales).[10] The sixth category (17 works) has yielded more than half of the comparative materials for the present book.

Aristides is a very difficult author (except in his diary, out of which he compiled the Sacred Tales). He tries to imitate his ideal, Demosthenes, and occasionally Isocrates, but his language is more obscure as a result of a studied and affected diction and elliptical phrasing. From his works he appears as "an unpleasantly vain and neurotic man." [11] Several psychiatrists have already devoted attention to the Sacred Tales because of the interesting materials of the dreams therein.[12] From a religio-historical point of view, these *Hieroi Logoi* and also the prose hymns to the gods (Zeus, Athena, Poseidon, Asclepius, Sarapis, etc.) are very important since they give us valuable insights into the personal religiosity of a man in this "age of anxiety" (Dodds).[13]

---

[7] These treatises were edited anew by W. Schmid in 1926 (see Bibl.).

[8] Both these orations are by the Byzantine monk Thomas Magister and were published by F. W. Lenz in his *Fünf Reden Thomas Magisters*, Leiden 1963.

[9] *Aristides* I (Loeb), p. XV.

[10] The titles of the orations can be found in the first index of the present book. The chronological order of the orations is to be found in Behr's *Aelius Aristides and the Sacred Tales* 128-130.

[11] Behr, *ibid.* 115.

[12] See in addition to the studies by the psychiatrists mentioned on p. 1 n. 2, the article by E. D. Phillips, A Hypochondriac and His God, *Greece and Rome* 21 (1952), 23-36.

[13] See, for example, the chapter on Aristides in A.-J. Festugière's *Personal Religion Among the Greeks*, Berkeley 1954. The Sacred Tales are accessible in the English translation by Behr in his *Aelius Aristides and the Sacred Tales* 205-292. Suggestions for improvements of this translation were made by Festugière in Sur les 'Discours Sacrés' d'Aelius Aristide, *Revue des études grecques* 82 (1969), 117-153.

The present collection of parallels

Although in this compilation the parallels between religious ideas in Aristides and the N.T. occupy a large place, all kinds of other parallels have been quoted too. There are stylistic parallels, grammatical parallels, ethical parallels, and historical parallels; lexical parallels have only been given in a few instances, since Walter Bauer has already gone through Aristides for this purpose. The parallels have mostly not been commented upon or evaluated. It is often hard to determine their value as long as only a very few authors from this period have been worked through in the same way. It is only in combination with similar compilations from many other authors that it is possible to assess what the parallels adduced are worth. Only then will it become clear which of them can stand criticism and which can not. Perhaps it should be stressed here that similarities in wording or phrasing or ideas do not imply some form of mutual dependency between Aristides and the N.T. None of the authors of the N.T. could have known the works of Aristides, and the orator does not show any knowledge of the N.T.

It is to be noted here that there is a most striking series of parallels to several Johannine passages about the relation between Christ and God. In Aristides' hymn to the goddess Athena, there are a number of lines on the relation between Athena and Zeus which parallel these passages in John, and also some in Paul and Hebrews; see the parallels adduced *ad* John I 18 (thrice); IX 4; X 18; XV 5; XVII 11 and 22; 1 Cor. I 24; Phil. II 6; Hebr. I 4; VI 20; see also *ad* Matt. XXVI 64.

As might be expected, there are also a large number of parallels to the Areopagus speech in Acts XVII 22-31. Further I would like to draw attention to the parallels to the use of καὶ in Acts V 29 and to the use of τί κωλύει in Acts VIII 31; also to the motif of vicarious dying in Mk. X 45b, John XI 50 and Rom. V 6-8. Other subjects can easily be found by way of the select index of subjects.

In order to clarify the system of references to Aristides the following remarks are provided. The latest complete edition (including the scholia) is by W. Dindorf in 1829 (repr. 1964). As early as in the nineteenth century it was recognized that this edition badly needed revision. Bruno Keil set himself this enormous task, and in 1898 the second volume of this edition, containing the orations 17-53 (according to his new numbering), was published; but the first volume never appeared. In 1926 the project was resumed by F. W. Lenz, who prepared a new edition of orations 1-16. When Lenz died in 1969, the editing of orations 1 and 5-16 had been completed. Now C. A. Behr is continuing this task by preparing a full-scale critical edition of all the works of Aristides and the scholia. The work started appearing in 1976. By now the first 8 orations have been published in 3 fascicles.

It stands to reason that the reference system used in my book should be the one used by Behr. Keil had already numbered the orations in another way than Dindorf had, and added paragraph numbers; Behr adopted this system of Keil. But since only the first 8 orations have been published so far, his numbering and paragraphing of the other orations has been kindly put to my disposal by Prof. Behr, so that the references found in my book are those of the newest critical edition. However, because this edition has as yet been only partly published, and Dindorf is still the only complete edition available, the references to the Dindorf edition have always been added in brackets. E.g. Ael. Arist. 11, 20 (33, p. 618) means: oration 11, paragraph 20 according to the new numbering by Behr, which is equivalent to oration 33, page 618 in Dindorf's edition. The author is very grateful to Prof. Behr for enabling him to give readers the newest reference system for Aristides, which will become standard for many decades to come.

PARALLELS

MATTHEW

Mt. I and II (σημεῖα on the occasion of Jesus' birth; cf. Lk. I and II, esp. II 12 τοῦτο ὑμῖν τὸ σημεῖον): Ael. Arist. 40, 2 (5, p. 53) καὶ τὰ σημεῖα εὐθὺς ἠκολούθησεν, sc. at Heracles' birth.

Mt. I 1 (γένεσις 'I. Χρ., I 18): Ael. Arist. 47, 73 (23, p. 463) ... ποιῆσαι μέλη, γάμον τε Κορωνίδος καὶ γένεσιν τοῦ θεοῦ. 1, 360 (13, p. 307) ἡ τῶν θεῶν γένεσις (sc. of Dionysus and Heracles). 21, 3 (22, p. 440) Διός τινα γένεσιν.

Mt. I 20 (γεννάω used of God; Joh. I 13; Acts XIII 33; 1 John passim): Ael. Arist. 28, 90 (49, p. 521) ... ὥσπερ τὸ αὐτὸ ποιοῦν εἰκόνα τε Ἑλένης καὶ τὸν Δία Ἑλένην αὐτὴν γεννῆσαι. 37, 2 (2, p. 13) γεννᾷ τε καὶ τίκτει τὴν θεόν (= Ἀθηνᾶν). 43, 16 (1, p. 6) Ἔρωτά τε καὶ Ἀνάγκην ... ἐν τοῖς πρῶτα ἐγγέννησεν (Ζεύς). Cf. also James I 18.

Mt. I 20 (II 12f., Acts XXIII 11, etc.): Ael. Arist. 28, 116 (49, p. 528) ἔχω δέ σοι καὶ λόγον τινὰ ἱερὸν διελθεῖν, ἀκούσας νύκτωρ οὐ πάλαι παρά του τῶν κρειττόνων, οἷόν ἐστι τὸ χρῆμα τῆς θείας μανίας. 50, 97 (26, p. 530) ἐγένοντο δέ μοι καὶ παρὰ τοῦ Σαράπιδος καὶ τῆς Ἴσιδος χρησμοί, ὡς πεπραξομένου τε τοῦ πράγματος. For the expression κατ' ὄναρ in Mt. I 20 etc. (only in Mt.) cf. Ael. Arist. 47, 21 (23, p. 450) κατὰ ὄναρ. On God-sent dreams in general see 47, 7 (23, p. 446) and 50, 39f. (26, pp. 513f.).

Mt. I 20 (God as κύριος): the title κύριος for a god occurs very seldom in Greek literature, but very often in the N.T.: Ael. Arist. 23, 79 (42, p. 795) τοῖς τῶν ὅλων κυρίοις ὁμοιοῦντες ἑαυτοὺς τοῖς θεοῖς. Cf. 42, 13 (6, p. 69).

Mt. I 20 (φαίνεσθαι of angels): Ael. Arist. 38, 28 (7, p. 78) φαίνεσθαι of oracle-gods.

Mt. I 21 (etymology of names; cf. XVI 18 Πέτρος-πέτρα): Ael. Arist. 47, 51f. (23, p. 458) ἐδόκουν ... τινὰ ἐλθεῖν, βιβλίον τι κομίζοντα τῶν Μενάνδρου. ... τοῦ θεοῦ μένειν προειρηκότος (Keil *ad loc.*: nomen omen τοῦ μένειν). 50, 21 (26, p. 508) ὁ Ῥώσανδρος δύναται δηλοῦν τὸν θεόν (Rosander, 'Man-Strengthener', has the equivalent meaning of the God).

Mt. I 21 (σῴζειν used of God and Christ; passim in the N.T.): Ael. Arist. 37, 17 (2, p. 21) Athena ἔτι νῦν σῴζει πάντας. 43, 1 (1, p. 1) Ζεῦ βασιλεῦ τε καὶ σῶτερ, ... ἔσωσας εὐμενῶς. 48, 37 (24, p. 474) αὐτὸς (sc. Asclepius) ἦν ὁ σῴζων, ..., μᾶλλον δὲ καὶ νῦν αὐτός ἐστιν ὁ σῴζων.

Mt. II 2 (7, 9, 10; stars as God-sent signs): Ael. Arist. 49, 39 (25, p. 498) ἔδοξα γὰρ ἑστῶτί μοι παρ' αὐτὸν τὸν βωμὸν τοῦ Διὸς ἐν τῇ ἀγορᾷ καὶ δεομένῳ φῆναι σημεῖον εἰ λῷον θῦσαι, ἀστέρα λαμπρὸν διᾷξαι δι' ἀγορᾶς κυροῦντα τὴν θυσίαν. οὕτω θαρρήσας ἔθυσα.

Mt. II 5 (οὕτω γὰρ γέγραπται, et passim): Ael. Arist. 11, 20 (33, p. 618) γέγραπται γὰρ ἐν αὐτῇ (sc. in the peace-treatise of Antalcidas) δή που τοὺς τὴν 'Ασίαν αὐτὴν οἰκοῦντας Ἕλληνας ὅ τι ἂν βούληται βασιλεὺς ἐξεῖναι δρᾶσαι.

Mt. II 12 (II 22, Lk. II 26, Acts X 22, Hebr. XII 25; χρηματίζειν): Ael. Arist. 48, 7 (24, p. 466) ἐνταῦθα πρῶτον ὁ Σωτὴρ χρηματίζειν ἤρξατο. Cf. 48, 71 (24, p. 484) καί μοι χρήζει ὁ θεὸς τὸ ἔπος τόδε, sc. in a dream. The χρηματισθῆναι in Mt. II 12 and 22 occurs also κατ' ὄναρ.

Mt. II 13: Ael. Arist. 2, 71 (45, p. 23) τὸ θεοὺς ἀνθρώπων κήδεσθαι ποιεῖ καὶ δι' ὀνειράτων ἀνθρώπους σῴζεσθαι.

Mt. II 13ff.: Oliver, *The Civilizing Power* 100, unnecessarily sees an allusion to this story of the flight to Egypt in the following words in Ael. Arist. 1, 25 (13, p. 163) οὐ γὰρ πλάνην καταλύσαντες οὐδὲ ὥσπερ ἐπὶ σκότους πατρίδα ζητοῦντες διὰ πάσης γῆς καὶ θαλάττης ... κατέσχον τὴν χώραν.

Mt. III 12 (Mk. IX 42, Lk. III 17): Ael. Arist. 26, 99 (14, p. 365) πῦρ ... ἄσβεστον.

Mt. IV 23 (et passim; healings by Jesus): Ael. Arist. 45, 29 (8, p. 95) οὗτος (= Σάραπις) κειμένους ἀνέστησεν. 38, 8 (7, p. 73) οὐδ' ἦν νοσεῖν ὅπου φανείη Μαχάων ἢ Ποδαλείριος. 38, 24 (7, p. 80) (said to the Asclepiads) ... τῆς τε νόσου παύετε καὶ διδοίητε ὑγιείας τε ὅσον οἷς ἡ ψυχὴ βούλεται τὸ σῶμα ὑπακούειν. 36, 124 (48, p. 489) τῶν ἰαμάτων ἀπὸ τῶν σωτήρων θεῶν ἀπολαύομεν ... ἡμᾶς βούλονται σῴζειν καὶ ὑγιεῖς ποιεῖν. 40, 12 (5, p. 59) νόσων τε ἁπασῶν ἐκλύεται (sc. Heracles; cf. ibid. 21 (p. 62)).

Mt. IV 24 (cf. VIII 6; healing of painful diseases); Ael. Arist. 42, 7 (6, p. 67) (on Asclepius) πολλὰς ὀδύνας τε καὶ ἀλγηδόνας καὶ ἀπορίας μεθημερινάς τε καὶ νυκτερινὰς ἀφεῖλεν πολλοῖς.

Mt. V 9 (Lk. XX 36, John I 12, XI 52, Rom. VIII 16, etc.: children of God): Ael. Arist. 1, 38 (13, p. 168) (on the Athenians) καίτοι πῶς οὐκ ἀληθῶς ἐκεῖνοι θεῶν μὲν παῖδες, θεῶν δὲ καὶ τρόφιμοι.

Mt. V 16 (et passim: ὁ πατὴρ ὑμῶν); Ael. Arist. 43, 6 (1, p. 2) τὸν ὑμέτερον ... πατέρα (sc. Zeus).

Mt. V 17 (καταλῦσαι τὸν νόμον): Ael. Arist. 37, 27 (2, p. 27) καταλύσαντα τοὺς μύθους.

Mt. V 18: Ael. Arist. 45, 18 (8, p. 89) ἐκ μὲν θεῶν οἴκων οὐδὲ ἐξέρχεται, οὐ πρότερόν γε ἢ ἄστρα τε ἐξ οὐρανοῦ καὶ αὐτὸς ὁ οὐρανὸς ἐξέλθοι ποτ' ἂν τῆς αὑτοῦ χώρας.

Mt. V 19 (ἐντολαί, sc. of God; passim in N.T.): Ael. Arist. 37, 6 (2, p. 15) τὰς ἐντολάς, sc. of Zeus.

Mt. V 20 (περισσεύσῃ ... ἡ δικαιοσύνη): Ael. Arist. 40, 6 (5, p. 55) δικαιοσύνης δὲ ὑπερβολῇ.

Mt. V 22 (συνέδριον, et passim): Ael. Arist. 50, 103 (26, p. 531) ἐν τῷ συνεδρίῳ τῷ κοινῷ (the provincial council of Asia Minor). 1, 301 (13, p. 286) ... ὥστε καταστῆναι τὴν πόλιν συνέδριον τῆς συμμαχίας ἁπάσης (Oliver: meeting place of the whole alliance; Behr: headquarters of ...; scholia: τουτέστι βουλευτήριον). For more passages see Oliver's Index s.v.

Mt. V 23f. (δῶρα προσφέρειν, Hebr. V 1, VIII 3.4, IX 9): Ael. Arist. 43, 1 (1, p. 1) σοὶ ..., Ζεῦ ..., δῶρα ἀνάγομεν.

Mt. V 25 (μήποτέ σε παραδῷ ὁ ἀντίδικος τῷ κριτῇ καὶ ὁ κριτὴς τῷ ὑπηρέτῃ): Ael. Arist. 2, 225 (45, p. 68) ὁ μὲν γὰρ ἐλέγχει τἀδικήματα ὁ ῥήτωρ καὶ παραδίδωσι τῷ δικαστῇ, ὁ δ' ἀκούσας καὶ μαθὼν παραδίδωσιν αὖ τοῖς ὑπηρέταις.

Mt. V 45 (τὸν ἥλιον αὐτοῦ ἀνατέλλει, sc. God): Ael. Arist. 43, 24 (1, p. 9) καὶ ἡ ἡλίου ἄπαυστος κίνησις ὑπὲρ γῆς τε καὶ ὑπὸ γῆν Διός ἐστι πρόρρησις ἡλίῳ προειρημένη ὑπὲρ τῆς τοῦ παντὸς κόσμου φανότητος.

Mt. V 48 (τέλειος): Ael. Arist. 1, 43 (13, p. 170) καὶ ζεύγνυσιν ἐν τῇδε τῇ γῇ πρῶτος ἀνθρώπων ὁ τῆσδε τῆς θεοῦ πάρεδρος (sc. 'Ερεχθεύς) ἅρμα τέλειον σὺν τῇ θεῷ καὶ φαίνει πᾶσι τὴν τελείαν ἱππικήν. 1, 45 (13, p. 170) the gods gave preliminary instruction to the Athenians, ἵν' ὥσπερ πανταχοῦ τῶν ἄκρων προδιδαξάντων καλῶς ἔχει τοῖς ζηλοῦσιν, οὕτω κἀκεῖνοι τέλειοι τὴν γιγνομένην ἀρετὴν ἀποβαῖεν. 26, 106 (14, p. 368) εἰ ὁμοίως Ὁμήρῳ τέλειος ἦν τὰ ποιητικὰ καὶ μαντικός (sc. Hesiod). 27, 21 (16, p. 390f.) ταῦτα μὲν οὖν οὐδὲν δεῖ λόγῳ κοσμεῖν, ἀλλ' εἰς τοὺς γεωμέτρας καὶ ἐπαΐοντας ἀποθέσθαι, καὶ τούτων ὅσοι τέλειοι καὶ ἱκανοὶ μετρῆσαι πρᾶγμα τοσοῦτον.

Mt. V 48 (ὁ πατὴρ ὁ οὐράνιος, in the N.T. 7 times only in Mt.): Ael. Arist. 43, 30 (1, p. 11) (Ζεὺς) οὐράνιος. Ibid. Zeus as πατήρ.

Mt. VI 2 (ἀπέχειν = εἰληφέναι): Ael. Arist. 12, 57 (34, p. 664) οὐχὶ νομίζω τοῖς ἀπέχειν τὴν δίκην ἡμᾶς τὴν παρὰ Λακεδαιμονίων φάσκουσιν εἶναι ταῦτα λέγειν. ... πῶς λέγουσιν εἰληφέναι τὴν δίκην ἡμᾶς;

Mt. VI 25 (οὐχὶ ἡ ψυχὴ πλεῖόν ἐστι τῆς τροφῆς καὶ τὸ σῶμα τοῦ ἐνδύματος): Ael. Arist. 2, 115 (45, p. 37) ... ὥσπερ ἂν εἴ τις τὰ ὑποδήματα κρείττω τῶν ποδῶν, τὴν δ' ἐσθῆτα τοῦ σώματος κρίνοι τιμιωτέραν. 23, 69 (42, p. 792) πάντων δὲ κάλλιστον ὑπάρχει πρὸς εὐθυμίαν αὐτοῖς· οὐ γὰρ ἡγοῦνται προσθήκην αὐτοὺς εἶναι τῶν ὑπαρχόντων, ἀλλὰ πάνθ' ὅσα ἂν κτήσωνται δεύτερα ἑαυτῶν εἶναι νομίζουσιν.

Mt. VI 25-32 (par.): Ael. Arist. 43, 19 (1, p. 7) τῆς δὲ ἐξ αὐτῶν (sc. the gods) προνοίας οὐδὲν πλέον ἢ ἄνθρωπον μετέχειν ἐποίησε (sc. Ζεύς). Cf. 50, 36 (26, p. 512). The N.T. never uses the word πρόνοια of God.

Mt. VI 26: Ael. Arist. 45, 32 (8, p. 96) (Sarapis) προέστηκε δὲ καὶ πάντων ζῴων γενέσεως καὶ τροφῆς.

Mt. VI 26 (X 31, XII 12; par.): Ael. Arist. 46, 10 (3, p. 32) καὶ μὴν ἄνθρωπός γε τί μὲν τῶν δένδρων διέφερεν τῶν ἐν τῇ γῇ αὐτοφυῶν.

Mt. VII 11 (et passim; οἶδα + inf. in the sense of "to be able"): Ael. Arist. 43, 19 (1, p. 8) ἀρχεῖν εἰδότι.

Mt. VII 22 (XXII 29, Acts II 22, et passim; δυνάμεις/δύναμις of Jesus and God): Ael. Arist. 42, 4 (6, p. 64) Ἀσκληπιοῦ δυνάμεις. See *ad* Mt. XXII 29.

Mt. VII 28 (XIII 54, etc.; ἔκπληξις after words and deeds of Jesus): Ael. Arist. 48, 15 (24, p. 469) ἔκπληξις as a reaction of outsiders to the marvellous deeds of the deity. 49, 45 (25, p. 500) ὡς δ' ἔγνω τὸ πᾶν, ἐξεπλάγη τε καὶ προσκυνήσας δίδωσιν (reaction to a miracle wrought by Isis).

Mt. VIII 26 (par.): Ael. Arist. 45, 29 (8, p. 95) οὗτος (Σάραπις) κύριος "ἠμὲν παυέμεναι ἠδ' ὀρνύμεν ὅν κ' ἐθέλῃσιν" (sc. ἄνεμον; *Od.* X 22). 38, 24 (7, p. 80) πολλὰς μὲν ἤδη τρικυμίας κατεπαύσατε (said to the Asclepiads). 42, 10 (6, p. 68) αὐτοῖς πλέουσι καὶ θορυβουμένοις φανεὶς ὁ θεὸς χεῖρα ὤρεξεν.

Mt. VIII 28-34: Ael. Arist. 1, 48 (13, p. 172) ... καὶ τυχὼν τῆς θεοῦ τῶν μανιῶν ἀπαλλάττεται (sc. Orestes).

Mt. IX 6 (par.; Eph. VI 21; 1 John V 13; ἵνα δὲ εἰδῆτε ὅτι ...): Ael. Arist. 28, 18 (49, p. 496) ἵνα τοίνυν εἰδῇς ὅτι ... Esp. 29, 9 (40, p. 754) ἵνα δὲ εἰδῆτε ὅτι ..., after a question as in Mt. IX 6. Cf. 11, 27 (33, p. 622).

Mt. IX 23 (combination of θόρυβος/θορυβέω and ὄχλος/λαός; cf. Acts XVII 5, XXIV 18; Mt. XXVI 5; Mk. XIV 2): Ael. Arist. 51, 13 (27, p. 537) πάντα ἦν θορύβου μεστὰ καὶ πλήθους ἀνθρώπων.

Mt. IX 33 (θαυμάζειν after healings; XV 31, Mk. V 20, Lk. XI 14; etc.): Ael. Arist. 47, 67 (23, p. 462) ... καὶ ἐθαύμαζον ὑπερφυῶς (after a healing). 51, 48 (27, p. 546) θαυμαστῶς ὡς ὁ θεὸς καὶ ἅμα εἰωθότως ἰάσατο.

Mt. X 19 (par., cf. Acts II 4): Ael. Arist. 45, 14 (8, p. 87) δὸς λέξαι τὸν λόγον εὐμενῶς (said to Sarapis). 45, 16 (8, p. 88) δίδωσι λέγειν αὐτός. 43, 1 (1, p. 1) τῷ λόγῳ ἐπάρκεσον (said to Zeus). 43, 31 (1, p. 11) παντὸς λόγου ... βοηθόν (Zeus). Cf. 42, 11 (6, p. 68) (on Asclepius) μαθήματα δὲ ἡμῖν γε καὶ λόγους ὑπέθηκε καὶ πρὸς τούτοις ἐννοήματα αὐτὰ καὶ τὴν λέξιν.

Mt. XI 29 (πραΰς εἰμι, 2 Cor. X 1): Ael. Arist. 39, 5 (18, p. 409) θεῶν ὁ πραότατός τε καὶ φιλανθρωπότατος (on God's φιλανθρωπία see *ad* Titus III 4).

Mt. XI 29 (ταπεινός, passim, nearly always *in bonam partem*): [Ael. Arist.] 25, 13 (43, p. 802) οὐδὲν ἂν πράξας ἀγεννὲς οὐδὲ ταπεινόν, and other passages, nearly always *in malam partem*.

Mt. XII 1ff. par.: Ael. Arist. 3, 445 (46, p. 326) οὐκοῦν εἰ μὲν τὰ τῶν ὁμιλητῶν ἁμαρτήματα τῶν προεστηκότων ἐστὶ κατηγορήματα, σαυτοῦ καὶ τοῦ ἑταίρου μᾶλλον κατηγόρηκας ἢ Περικλέους κτλ. See D. Daube, "Responsibility of Master and Disciples in the Gospels", *NTS* 19 (1972), 1-15.

Mt. XII 12 (cf. VI 26, X 31; Lk. XII 7.24): Ael. Arist. 43, 17 (1, p. 7) τὰ δὲ μέσα ὅσα τε ἀέρος καὶ θαλάττης θρέμματα καὶ ὅσα λοιπὰ γῆς, ὑπ' ἀμφοτέροις (sc. θεοῖς καὶ ἀνθρώποις) ἐποίησεν (sc. Ζεύς).

Mt. XII 38 (et passim; σημεῖα for the miraculous deeds of Jesus): Ael. Arist. 40, 2 (5, p. 53) σημεῖα for the miraculous deeds of Heracles.

Mt. XII 40 (ἐν τῇ καρδίᾳ τῆς γῆς): Ael. Arist. 37, 9 (2, p. 16) ἐκ τῶν κοίλων τῆς γῆς.

Mt. XII 42 (par.; Rom. X 18; τὰ πέρατα τῆς γῆς): Ael. Arist. 1, 66 (13, p. 183) καὶ νῦν ἐπ' ἀμφοτέροις τοῖς πέρασι τῆς γῆς ὑμετέρων παίδων παῖδες οἰκοῦσιν, οἱ μὲν ἄχρι Γαδείρων (Cadiz) ἀπὸ Μασσαλίας (Marseilles) παρήκοντες, οἱ δ' ἐπὶ τῷ Τανάϊδι (Don) καὶ τῇ Λίμνῃ (Sea of Azov) μεμερισμένοι. Cf. also 26, 28 (14, p. 334) and 46, 10 (3, 32).

Mt. XIII 13 (par.; βλέποντες οὐ βλέπουσιν καὶ ἀκούοντες οὐκ ἀκούουσιν): Ael. Arist. 3, 225 (46, p. 246) ... καὶ μήτ' ἀκούοντας ἀκούειν τὰ δεινὰ μήθ' ὁρῶντας ὁρᾶν. For the combination of seeing and hearing (also in John III 32, Acts XIX 26, 2 Ptr. II 8, 1 John I 1.3) see also 46, 10 and 40 (3, pp. 32 and 46).

Mt. XIII 43 etc. (ὁ ἔχων ὦτα ἀκούειν): Ael. Arist. 28, 113 (49, p. 528) ἐν μύθῳ τις ἀπόρρητος λόγος τοῖς μὲν ἀκούειν δυνατοῖς εἰρήσεται.

Mt. XIII 47 (Mk. I 17f. par.): Ael. Arist. 26, 85 (14, p. 358) Darius μίαν πόλιν ἠδυνήθη σαγηνεύσας ἑλεῖν, ὑμεῖς δ' ἅπασαν, εἰ οἷόν τε εἰπεῖν, σαγηνεύσαντες τὴν οἰκουμένην κτλ.

Mt. XIV 25 (par.): Ael. Arist. 1, 85 (13, p. 191) (The Thracians wanted to defeat the Athenians) ἔγνωσαν παραπλήσια βουλεύσαντες ὥσπερ ἂν εἰ τὴν θάλατταν ἐνεχείρουν περαιοῦσθαι πεζῇ (walking on the sea = doing something impossible). 46, 19 (3, p. 36) ἄνωθεν ἐπὶ τῶν κυμάτων ἐπιθέοντα (Poseidon).

Mt. XIV 30 (σῴζω in the sense of "to save from peril of life"; XXVII 40.42; Acts XXVII 20, etc.): Ael. Arist. 47, 71 (23, p. 463) ἐδεόμην σῶσαί μοι τὸν Ζώσιμον.

Mt. XV 19 ("Lasterkatalog", passim in the N.T.): Ael. Arist. 37, 27 (2, p. 27) ἀφροσύνη μὲν καὶ ἀσέλγεια καὶ δειλία καὶ ἀταξία καὶ στάσις καὶ ὕβρις και ὑπερηφανία (all these words occur also in the N.T. as sins).

Mt. XVI 18 (πύλαι ᾅδου): Ael. Arist. 49, 4 (25, p. 489) πύλῃσιν ... Ἀΐδεω.

Mt. XVI 19 (τὰς κλεῖδας τῆς βασιλείας τῶν οὐρανῶν): Ael. Arist. 45, 24 (8, p. 92) γῆς καὶ θαλάττης, φαῖεν ἂν ποιηταί, κληῖδας ἔχων (sc. Sarapis).

Mt. XVI 21 (δεῖ/ἔδει of divine necessity; Lk. XXIV 26, Acts I 16): Ael. Arist. 1, 67 (13, p. 183) ἐπεὶ δὲ ἔδει τὴν Πελοπόννησον τῶν Δωριέων γενέσθαι, ... (Behr: when it was fated that ...). Cf. 48, 26 (24, p. 472) ἔφη χρῆναι τελευτᾶν εἰς τρίτην ἡμέραν καὶ ταῦτα ἀναγκαίως ἔχειν (cf. χρῆναι τελευτᾶν with δεῖ ... ἀποκτανθῆναι in Mt.).

Mt. XVI 28 (par.; Hebr. VI 4f. γεύομαι metaph.): Ael. Arist. 28, 60 (49, p. 510) ... τὸ λεγόμενον δὴ τοῦτο ἐπὶ γήραος οὐδῷ γευόμενος τῆς ἀλαζονείας.

Mt. XVII 21 (par., τοῦτο τὸ γένος for demons): Ael. Arist. 37, 9 (2, p. 15) the Giants ἦσαν .. ἀπ' ἐναντίου τοῦ γένους αὐτῇ (sc. Athena).

Mt. XVIII 15 (ἁμαρτάνω, passim): Ael. Arist. 2, 139-140 (45, p. 43) (from this passage it is clear that in non-biblical Greek ἁμαρτάνω has retained the sense of "missing the mark") ὡς οἵ γ' ἀποτυγχάνοντες ἀρχὴν οὐδὲ στοχάζονται, ἀλλ' αὐτὸ τοὐναντίον τῷ στοχάζεσθαι ποιοῦσιν. τὸ γὰρ στοχάζεσθαι τοῦτ' ἐστὶ τυχεῖν τοῦ πράγματος. οὐκοῦν οὐχ ᾧ στοχάζεται ἁμαρτάνει τις, ἀλλ' ᾧ διήμαρτεν οὐκ ἐστοχάσατο. εἰκότως· οὐδεὶς γὰρ ἁμαρτάνει λόγῳ χρώμενος, ἀλλ' ἅμα ἐσφάλη καὶ τὸν λόγον οὐ διεσώσατο. ὁ γὰρ λόγος ταύτην εἶχε τὴν δύναμιν, μὴ διαμαρτάνειν, καὶ τοῦθ' οὕτως ἀληθές ἐστιν ὥστε οἱ φρονιμώτατοι τῶν ἀνθρώπων καὶ λόγου πλείστου μετέχοντες ἄριστα στοχάζονται.

Mt. XVIII 20: Ael. Arist. 45, 27 (8, p. 94) Sarapis is συμποσιάρχου τάξιν ἔχων τοῖς ἀεὶ κατ' αὐτὸν συλλεγομένοις.

Mt. XIX 19 (= Lev. XIX 18; par., etc.): Ael. Arist. 3, 339 (46, p. 288) ἡ μὲν οὖν τοῦ πρωτείου ψῆφος, οἶμαι, τοῦ φύσει πᾶσιν ἀνθρώποις συμβεβηκότος ἦν, τοῦτο δ' ἐστὶ μηδένα ἑαυτοῦ μᾶλλον φιλεῖν.

Mt. XIX 29 (par.): Ael. Arist. 16, 13 (52, p. 590f.) ... πῶς οὖν ἐμέ γ' εἰκὸς καταλιπόντα τὴν ἐμαυτοῦ γυναῖκα καὶ πρὸς τῇ γυναικὶ παῖδας καὶ γονεῖς ἐν γήρᾳ καὶ χρήματα καὶ οἰκέτας πλεῖν ἔξω τῆς Ἑλλάδος, καὶ πρὸς τούτοις ἔτι κινδυνεύειν ἐπὶ στρατείας περὶ ψυχῆς....

Mt. XX 8 (ἀπόδος αὐτοῖς τὸν μισθόν, cf. Apoc. XI 18): Ael. Arist. 37, 4 (2, p. 14) ἀποδιδοῦσα πρέποντα τὸν μισθόν. For this use of ἀποδιδόναι = to give or render what is due, see 1, 80 (13, p. 188): when the Thebans did not allow the corpses of their adversaries to be buried, the Athenians intervened and πρέπουσαν τοῖς μὲν τὴν τιμήν, τοῖς δὲ τὴν τιμωρίαν ἀπέδοσαν (*scholia ad loc.*: εἰκότως ἔχει τὸ ἀπέδοσαν· ἄξιοι γὰρ Θηβαῖοι μὲν τιμωρίας, ὡς ἀνόσιοι, Ἀργεῖοι δὲ τιμῆς, ὡς ἀδίκως ῥιφέντες. διὸ καὶ ἀμφότεροι τῶν ὀφειλομένων ἔτυχον). Cf. also 1, 149 (13, p. 224).

Mt. XX 28 (οὐκ ἦλθεν διακονηθῆναι ἀλλὰ διακονῆσαι, cf. Lk. XXII 26f.): Ael. Arist. 2, 387 (45, p. 130) ὅσῳ γὰρ βέλτιον ἄρχειν ἢ διακονεῖν, τοσούτῳ λέγειν τὰ δέοντα βέλτιον ἢ πράττειν.

Mt. XXI 15 (τὰ θαυμάσια ἃ ἐποίησεν): Ael. Arist. 40, 12 (5, p. 59) θαυμαστὰ οἷα ἐργάζεται (Heracles).

Mt. XXI 41 (κακοὺς κακῶς ἀπολέσει αὐτούς): Ael. Arist. 46, 33 (3, p. 43) τῶν κάκιστα ἀπολωλότων. *Ad* κακοὺς κακῶς (cf. Rom. XII 17, 1 Thess. V 15, 1 Ptr. III 9) cf. 46, 36 (3, p. 44) κακὰ γὰρ ἐκ κακῶν.

Mt. XXII 14 (God's call; Acts II 39, XIII 2, XVI 10; Rom. VIII 30, et passim): Ael. Arist. 23, 15 (42, p. 772) παρὰ τοῦ θεοῦ καλοῦντός τε ὡς αὐτόν.

Mt. XXII 23 (λέγοντες μὴ εἶναι ἀνάστασιν): Ael. Arist. 31, 16-18 (11, p. 131-132). According to Behr, *Aelius Aristides* 93f., it is apparent from passages like this one that "as many others of this age, Aristides had no belief in an after life"; cf. also 150 n. 10. (The passage is too long to be quoted in its entirety).

Mt. XXII 29 (par. ἡ δύναμις τοῦ θεοῦ): Ael. Arist. 41, 7 (4, p. 49) ἡ δύναμις τοῦ θεοῦ. The same expression in 23, 18 (42, p. 773); 37, 17 (2, p. 20); 48, 30 (24, p. 473).

Mt. XXII 31 (God speaking to people; Mk. XII 26, Lk. I 55, John IX 29, Hebr. XII 25): Ael. Arist. 46, 34 (3, p. 43) θεοὺς ... ἀνθρώποις διαλεγομένους.

Mt. XXIII 5: Ael. Arist. 1, 34 (13, p. 167) the Athenians thought that it was good εἰ πάντας εὖ ποιοῦντες ὀφθήσονται.

Mt. XXIV 6 (par., wars und rumours of wars): Ael. Arist. 26, 70 (14, p. 350f.) πόλεμοι δὲ ... ἀτεχνῶς ὥσπερ μῦθοι ταχέως αὐτοί τε παρῆλθον καὶ οἱ περὶ αὐτῶν λόγοι.

Mt. XXIV 6f.: Ael. Arist. 18, 7 (20, p. 427) πῦρ καὶ πόλεμοι καὶ σεισμοί.

Mt. XXIV 30 (φανήσεται τὸ σημεῖον): Ael. Arist. 48, 72 (24, p. 484) τοῦ θεοῦ σημεῖα φαίνοντος. For σημεῖα of God see e.g. Acts XV 12.

Mt. XXV 18, 25: Ael. Arist. 1, 34 (13, p. 167) the Athenians did not bury their riches, but they benefitted all men by it. οὐ γὰρ ἠξίωσαν αὐτὸ δὴ τοῦτο γῇ κρύψαντες ἐξαρκεῖν (*scholia ad loc.*: παροιμία ἐπὶ τῶν φθονούντων καὶ μὴ μεταδόντων τοῖς ἄλλοις τῶν παρὰ σφίσιν αὐτοῖς ἀγαθῶν τὸ "γῇ κρύψας ἔχῃ").

Mt. XXVI 42 etc. (ἐκ δευτέρου): Ael. Arist. 43, 20 (1, p. 8) ἐκ τῶν δευτέρων.

Mt. XXVI 64 (par., et passim: sitting at the right hand of God): Ael. Arist. 37, 6 (2, p. 15) δεξιὰν κατὰ χεῖρα τοῦ πατρὸς αὐτὴν καθεζομένην (sc. the goddess Athena).

Mt. XXVII 2 (Acts XXIII 24, et passim: ἡγεμών in the sense of "imperial provincial governor"): Ael. Arist. 50, 12 (26, p. 505) ἡγεμὼν τῆς 'Ασίας ... Σεβῆρος. See also 50, 71 (26, p. 523).

Mt. XXVII 19 (καθίζω/κάθημαι ἐπὶ τοῦ βήματος, of Pilate, as in John XIX 3; Acts XII 21 of Herodes; Acts XXV 6, 17 of Festus; Acts XXV 10 βῆμα Καίσαρος): Ael. Arist. 47, 23 (23, p. 451) καθέζεσθαι δ' αὐτὸν (sc. the Emperor) ἐπί τινος βήματος.

Mt. XXVIII 1 (par., εἷς instead of πρῶτος; John XX 1, Acts XX 7, 1 Cor. XVI 2): Ael. Arist. 50, 23 (26, p. 509) μίαν ἢ δευτέραν τινὰ ἡμέραν. 36, 40 (48, p. 453) ἕν ..., δεύτερον ..., τρίτον...

Mt. XXVIII 18 (ἐδόθη μοι πᾶσα ἐξουσία ἐν οὐρανῷ καὶ ἐπὶ γῆς): Ael. Arist. 37, 8 (2, p. 15) τὸ μὲν δὴ κράτος τῆς θεοῦ (sc. Athena) τοσοῦτον ἐν οὐρανῷ καὶ γῇ.

MARK

Mk. I 1 (ἀρχὴ τοῦ εὐαγγελίου): Ael. Arist. 23, 2 (42, p. 768) ἐπ' ἀρχῇ τοῦ συγγράμματος ...

Mk. I 2 (ἀποστέλλω with God as subject; John I 6, III 34, 1 John IV 9, et passim; with Jesus as subject, Lk. X 1, etc.): Ael. Arist. 50, 87 (26, p. 528) ... ὁ θεὸς αὐτῶν τούτων ἕνεκα ἀποστείλειεν (sc. Asclepius).

Mk. I 44 (μηδενὶ μηδέν, Rom. XIII 8, 2 Cor. VI 3): Ael. Arist. 2, 336 (45, p. 111) μηδὲν ἁμαρτάνειν μηδένας ἀνθρώπων μηδαμῇ. Cf. 43, 18 (1, p. 7) μηδαμοῦ μηδέν.

Mk. IV 11 (οἱ ἔξω, 1 Cor. V 12f., 2 Cor. IV 16, Col. IV 5, 1 Thess. IV 12): Ael. Arist. 2, 214 (45, p. 65) τοὺς ἔξω δεῖ πεῖσαι. 9, 13 (38, p. 715) οὔτε γὰρ τῆς ἀξίας τῆς ὑμετέρας τοὺς ἔξω θαυμάζειν ...

Mk. IV 20 (τὸν λόγον ... παραδέχονται): Ael. Arist. 36, 6 (48, p. 439) παραδεξόμεθα τοῦτον τὸν λόγον.

Mk. V 25-29 (par., John V 5-9): Ael. Arist. 38, 10 (7, p. 74) τὴν Φιλοκτήτου νόσον, ἣν Ὀδυσσεὺς καὶ Ἀτρεῖδαι προκαταγνόντες ἀνίατον εἶναι Φιλοκτήτην οὐχὶ δικαίως ἐν Λήμνῳ κατέλιπον, οὗτοι (sc. the Asclepiads Podalirius and Machaon) δὲ δέκα ἔτεσιν αὐξηθεῖσαν ἰάσαντο. 2, 67 (45, p. 22) ὑφ' ὧν (sc. θεῶν) ἃ μηδεὶς ἰατρῶν μήτε οἶδεν ὅ τι χρὴ προσειπεῖν, οὐχ ὅπως ἰάσασθαι, μήτε εἶδεν ἐν ἀνθρώπου φύσει συμβάντα, ἄλλοτε ἄλλαις παραμυθίαις τε καὶ συμβουλαῖς ἐκ τοῦ θεοῦ διαφεύγων ζῶ παρὰ πᾶν τὸ ἐκ τῶν παρόντων εἰκός. 47, 62 and 67 (23, pp. 461 and 462) ἐνταῦθα οἱ μὲν ἰατροὶ πάσας φωνὰς ἠφίεσαν, οἱ μὲν τέμνειν, οἱ δὲ ἐπικάειν φαρμάκοις, ἢ πάντως δεῖν ὑπόπυον γενόμενον διαφθαρῆναι. ... (67) ἐντεῦθεν δὲ ἤδη τῶν μὲν ἐγκλημάτων ἐπαύσαντο οἱ ἰατροὶ καὶ ἐθαύμαζον ὑπερφυῶς ἐφ' ἑκάστῳ τοῦ θεοῦ τὴν πρόνοιαν, καὶ ὡς ἕτερόν τι ἄρα ἦν μεῖζον, ὃ λάθρᾳ ἰᾶτο. See further *ad* Mk. V 26.

Mk. V 26 (par.): Ael. Arist. 48, 69 (24, p. 483) συνῆλθον οἵ τε ἰατροὶ καὶ γυμνασταὶ καὶ οὔτε βοηθεῖν εἶχον οὔτε ἐγνώριζον τὴν ποικιλίαν τῆς νόσου. 48, 39 (24, p. 475) καὶ οἱ ἰατροὶ ἀφίσταντο καὶ τελευτῶντες ἀπέγνωσαν παντάπασιν. See O. Weinreich, *Antike Heilungswunder* 195ff.

Mk. V 42: Ael. Arist. 50, 10 (26, p. 504) καὶ ἡ τροφὸς εὐθὺς ἀνειστήκει καὶ ἀπήντα καὶ ἔρρωτο. 47, 72 (23, p. 463) ἀνίσταται παρ' ἐλπίδας ἐξ ἐκείνης τῆς νόσου. 47, 78 (23, p. 464) κειμένην δέ ποτε ἀνέστησεν. For the use of ἀνίσταμαι after healings see also Mk. IX 27, Acts IX 40, XIV 10.

Mk. VI 13 (James V 14; healing by anointing): Ael. Arist. 49, 22 (25, p. 494) καὶ χρίομαι ὡς ἔτυχον προσεστώς. ἦν δὲ καὶ τὸ χρῖμα τῆς εὐωδίας θαυμαστὸν οἷον καὶ ἡ δύναμις εὐθὺς ἐπίδηλος. θᾶττον γὰρ ἢ εἴρηκα ἀνείθη ἡ τάσις.

Mk. VII 22 (ἀσέλγεια . . . ὑπερηφανία, ἀφροσύνη in a "Lasterkatalog"): Ael. Arist. 37, 27 (2, p. 27) ἀφροσύνη . . . ἀσέλγεια . . . ὑπερηφανία.

Mk. VIII 32 (et passim, παρρησία): Ael. Arist. 3, 118 (46, p. 198) Πλάτων εἶπε μὴ δεῖν κολακεύειν τὰ πλήθη· Περικλῆς δέ γε πλείστῃ παρρησίᾳ χρησάμενος φαίνεται (*scholion ad loc.* ἡ γὰρ παρρησία ἐναντία ἐστὶ τῇ κολακείᾳ· ἡ μὲν γὰρ κολακεία ἔχει τὸ ἡδύ, ἡ δὲ [παρρησία] καὶ τὸ λυπηρὸν πολλάκις).

Mk. IX 27 (ἀναστῆναι after illness, Lk. IV 39, V 25, Acts IX 40): Ael. Arist. 42, 6 (6, p. 66) εἰσὶν οἵ φασιν ἀναστῆναι κείμενοι (= ill).

Mk. IX 40 (par., ὃς γὰρ οὐκ ἔστιν καθ' ἡμῶν, ὑπὲρ ἡμῶν ἐστιν): Ael. Arist. 1, 235 (13, p. 263) . . . ὥσπερ ἁπάντων τούτων ὑπὲρ αὐτῶν, ἀλλ' οὐ κατ' αὐτῶν γιγνομένων.

Mk. X 27 (par., πάντα δυνατὰ παρὰ τῷ θεῷ, cf. Lk. I 37): Ael. Arist. 45, 14 (8, p. 87) πάντως οὐδέν γε σοὶ (sc. Σαράπιδι) ἀδύνατον.

Mk. X 45a: Ael. Arist. 3, 126 (46, p. 202) ὁρῶντες ἄνδρα (sc. Περικλέα) καὶ λέγειν καὶ πράττειν ἄκρον καὶ δουλείας μὲν οὐδαμῶς ἐγγύς, ἄρχειν δ' ἐπιτηδειότατον καὶ ἱκανώτατον καὶ πάντων ὑπερπεφυκότα τῶν ἄλλων, ἔπαθόν τι Ὁμηρικὸν καὶ παραπλήσιον αὐτὸν τοῖς θεοῖς ἐνόμισαν. Contrast also Phil. II 7!

Mk. X 45b: Ael. Arist. 51, 24 (27, p. 540) ἡ Φιλουμένη ψυχὴν ἀντὶ ψυχῆς καὶ σῶμα ἀντὶ σώματος ἀντέδωκεν, τὰ αὐτῆς ἀντὶ τῶν ἐμῶν (Aristides dreamt that the death of the girl Philoumene was on his behalf. See a strikingly similar dream of Carl Gustav Jung in *Erinnerungen, Träume, Gedanken* (ed. A. Jaffé,) Zürich 1962, 296f.

Mk. XII 29 (= Deut. VI 4; ὁ θεὸς . . . εἷς ἐστιν, et passim): Ael. Arist. 50, 50 (26, p. 518) ἐξεβόησα· 'εἷς', λέγων δὴ τὸν θεόν. 45, 23 (8, p. 91) οὗτος εἷς ὢν (sc. Σάραπις). 45, 24 (8, p. 92).

Mk. XIII 35 (XIV 30 par., *et al.*; cock-crow as indication of time): Ael. Arist. 50, 35 (26, p. 512) ἀλεκτρυόνων τε ᾠδαὶ πλησίον ἦσαν, καὶ καταρρήγνυται σκηπτός. 51, 5 (27, p. 535) ... περὶ ἀλεκτρυόνων μάλιστά πως ᾠδάς ...

Mk. XIV 3 (μύρου νάρδου πιστικῆς πολυτελοῦς, John XII 3 μύρου νάρδου πιστικῆς πολυτίμου): Ael. Arist. 49, 23 (25, p. 494) κρᾶσις (?, mss. κάθαρσις) τριῶν, ὁποῦ τε ᾧ χριόμεθα καὶ μύρου ναρδίνου καὶ ἑτέρου μύρου τῶν πολυτελῶν.

[Mk.] XVI 9 (ἐφάνη, cf. Mt. I 20): Ael. Arist. 47, 71 (23, p. 463) φανέντος δὲ τοῦ θεοῦ. Cf. 48, 9 (24, p. 467).

LUKE

Lk. I 1-4: Ael. Arist. 47, 3 (23, p. 445) εἴ τις παρὼν ἢ τὰ συμπίπτοντα ἀπογράφειν ἠβούλετο ἢ τὴν τοῦ θεοῦ πρόνοιαν διηγεῖσθαι (in a prooemium).

Lk. I 1 (πολλοὶ ἐπεχείρησαν ἀνατάξασθαι διήγησιν): Ael. Arist. 43, 2 (1, p. 1) μήτε ... μήτε ἐγχειρῆσαι (sc. ὕμνον ἐρεῖν) σωφροσύνης ... ἔχει πίστιν.

Lk. I 3 (ἀκριβῶς): Ael. Arist. 48, 1 (24, p. 465) χρόνου δὲ αὖ προελθόντος ἕν τι τῶν ἀδυνάτων εἶναι ἐδόκει καὶ μνημονεῦσαι ἕκαστα καὶ δι' ἀκριβείας εἰπεῖν (in a prooemium; this whole prooemium shows some similarity to Lk. I 1-4). 48, 18 (24, p. 470) καὶ τὰ μὲν κεφάλαια τῆς ἐπιφανείας ταῦτά ἐστιν, ὡς ἀντὶ τοῦ παντός γ' ἂν ἐποιησάμην καὶ τὰ καθ' ἕκαστα δύνασθαι δι' ἀκριβείας διεξελθεῖν. 51, 66 (27, p. 550) ἐδόκουν καλεῖν Εὔδοξον ὡς ἀπογραψόμενον διά τε τὸ μακρότερα εἶναι καὶ τὸ βούλεσθαι δι' ἀκριβείας αὐτῷ σῶσαι.

Lk. I 3 (καθεξῆς ... γράψαι): Ael. Arist. 50, 68 (26, p. 522) ἐπεὶ δ' ἐνταῦθα ἐγεγόνειν τοῦ λόγου καὶ πρὸς τὰς ἄλλας ἔμελλον εὐεργεσίας τοῦ θεοῦ τρέψεσθαι καὶ γράψειν ἐφεξῆς τὰς ἐπὶ τῶν ἄλλων ἡγεμόνων καὶ πραγμάτων γενομένας, ...

Lk. I 3 (κράτιστε Θεόφιλε, cf. Acts I 1): Ael. Arist. 51, 63 (27, p. 551) τοὺς μὲν νεὼς τοῖς θεοῖς προσήκει καθιεροῦν, τοὺς δὲ ἄνδρας τοὺς ἐλλογίμους τῇ τῶν βιβλίων ἀναθέσει τιμᾶν. Cf. 50, 16 (25, p. 506) ἀνὴρ τῶν ἐστρατηγηκότων Ῥωμαίοις ... Θεόφιλος.

Lk. I 8 (ἐν τῷ ἱερατεύειν αὐτὸν ἐν τῇ τάξει τῆς ἐφημερίας αὐτοῦ): Ael. Arist. 48, 47 (24, p. 477) οἵ τε γὰρ νεωκόροι ... καὶ πάντες οἱ περὶ τὸν θεὸν θεραπευταὶ καὶ τάξεις ἔχοντες ...

Lk. I 13 (εἰσηκούσθη ἡ δέησίς σου, cf. Acts X 31): Ael. Arist. 49, 49 (25, p. 501) πολλάκις ἤδη μοι ἐπὶ τῆς εὐχῆς ἦλθεν ἡ ἀπόκρισις.

Lk. I 23 (λειτουργία, 2 Cor. IX 12, Phil. II 17, 30, Hebr. VIII 6, IX 21; λειτουργέω, Acts XIII 2, Rom. XV 27, Hebr. X 11): Ael. Arist. 10, 38 (39, p. 747) τοῖς θεοῖς ..., οἷς ἡμεῖς τόνδε τὸν χρόνον λειτουργήσομεν. 49, 32 (25, p. 496) ὡς δὲ καὶ τοῦτο ἐλελειτούργητο (as commanded by the God). 49, 50 (25, p. 501) ἱκανῶς ὑμῖν, ὦ οὗτοι, λελειτούργηται, πορεύεσθε. In these instances λειτουργέω has a religious force; see A. J. Festugière in *Rev. Ét. Grecques* 82 (1969), 136f. This is not the case in 26, 75 (14, p. 352) ... ἐσκέψασθε τοὺς λειτουργήσοντας τήνδε τὴν λειτουργίαν, which is about military service.

Lk. I 26-33: Ael. Arist. 3, 97 (46, p. 191) ... Περικλέα, ὅν γε καὶ πρὶν γενέσθαι προσεῖπεν ἀπ' αὐτῶν τῶν ἐναντιωτάτων ὁ θεός, προειπὼν αὐτοῦ τῇ μητρὶ λέοντα τέξεσθαι· ἡ δ' ἐπὶ ταύτῃ τῇ ὄψει τίκτει Περικλέα.

Lk. I 28ff. (cf. v. 42): Ael. Arist. 40, 2 (5, p. 53) (on Heracles' mother) μήτηρ δὲ ἣν ἐκεῖνος (= Ζεὺς) ἐξ ἁπασῶν προὔκρινεν.

Lk. I 47 (σωτήρ for God or Jesus, passim, e.g. Acts XIII 23, 1 Tim. I 1): Ael. Arist. 50, 32 (26, p. 511) τῷ 'Απόλλωνι τῷ ... Σωτῆρι. 42, 4 (6, p. 64f.) Asclepius is σωτὴρ τῶν ὅλων ... σῴζων τά τε ὄντα ἀεὶ καὶ τὰ γιγνόμενα. 39, 3 (18, p. 409) τὸν σωτῆρα θεόν (Asclepius). 23, 14 (42, p. 772) τὸ τελευταῖον τμῆμα τῆς πόλεως, ὃ τῷ σωτῆρι καθωσίωται κατὰ τὴν κοινὴν ἁπάντων ἀνθρώπων ἀγαθὴν τύχην (sc. Asclepius in Pergamum). 43, 1 (1, p. 1) Ζεῦ ... σῶτερ. Cf. 43, 30 (1, p. 11).

Lk. I 49 (God as δυνατός, Hebr. XI 19): Ael. Arist. 37, 17 (2, p. 20) Athena is δυνατωτάτη.

Lk. I 50 (God's ἔλεος, passim): Ael. Arist. 45, 26 (8, p. 93) πρὸς δ' οὖν τὸν ἔλεον μᾶλλον τέτραπται (sc. Sarapis).

Lk. I 66 (God's hand, Acts IV 30, VII 25, XI 21, Hebr. X 31 plur.): Ael. Arist. 1, 298 (13, p. 285) the Thebans planned to destroy the Lacedaemonians, ὥστε δεῖν ... θεῶν τινα χεῖρα ὑπερέχειν ... 47, 42 (23, p. 455) ... τυγχάνειν ἀκηκοὼς ὡς, εἰ γενοίμην ἐν χερσὶ τοῦ θεοῦ, ἐλπίδες εἶεν. See also *ad* Acts IV 30.

Lk. I 71 (σωτηρία in the sense of the saving of human lives, Acts VII 25, XXVII 34, Hebr. XI 7): Ael. Arist. 43, 21 (1, p. 8) ἡ τοῦ βίου σωτηρία. 1, 55 (13, p. 177/8) and many other passages in this Panathenaic Oration, see Oliver's Index *s.v.* Cf. 46, 1 (3, p. 29).

Lk. I 71, 74 (God saves from the hands of the enemies): Ael. Arist. 37, 27 (2, p. 27) Athena ἡ τοὺς ... πολεμίους ἡμῶν ἀπείργουσα.

Lk. II 1 (πᾶσα ἡ οἰκουμένη, cf. also ὅλη ἡ οἰκουμένη, e.g. Mt. XXIV 14): Ael. Arist. 26, 9.29.33.36.59.61.97.101.102 (14, pp. 325.334f.

336.346.347.364.365f.); 44, 3 (17, p. 401); 39, 4 (18, p. 409); 1, 31 (13, p. 165); etc. See Oliver's Index *s.v.* One instance may suffice: 44, 3 (17, p. 401) ἐν γὰρ τῷ μέσῳ τῆς πάσης οἰκουμένης τε καὶ θαλάττης μάλιστα ἵδρυται (sc. τὸ Αἰγαῖον πέλαγος).

Lk. II 29 (God or Christ as δεσπότης, Acts IV 24, 2 Ptr. II 1, Jude 4, Apoc. VI 10): Ael. Arist. 42, 1 (6, p. 63) Ἀσκληπιὲ δέσποτα. 37, 1 (2, p. 12) ὦ δέσποινα Ἀθηνᾶ. Cf. 26, 23 (14, p. 332) where the Persian king is called βασιλεὺς καὶ δεσπότης (= master of slaves; see the whole chapter; cf. in the N.T. e.g. 1 Tim. VI 1f.).

Lk. II 37 (praying to God day and night, XVIII 7, Acts XXVI 7, 1 Thess. III 10, 1 Tim. V 5, Apoc. VII 15): Ael. Arist. 42, 1 (6, p. 63) ὦ πολλὰ δὴ πολλάκις ἐν νυξί τε καὶ ἡμέραις ἰδίᾳ τε καὶ δημοσίᾳ κληθεὶς ὑφ' ἡμῶν, Ἀσκληπιὲ δέσποτα.

Lk. II 40 (χάρις θεοῦ, passim): Ael. Arist. 47, 77 (23, p. 464) οὕτως ὅσον τε ἐπεβίω, χάρις ἦν τοῦ θεοῦ.

Lk. II 52 (ἐν ... χάριτι παρὰ θεῷ καὶ ἀνθρώποις): Ael. Arist. 45, 18 (8, p. 89) Sarapis ἔχει δύναμιν καὶ τιμὴν παρὰ θεοῖς καὶ ἀνθρώποις.

Lk. III 1 (ἡγεμονία of the emperor Tiberius, only here in the N.T.): Ael. Arist. 26, 10 (14, p. 326) τῆς ὑμετέρας ἡγεμονίας (sc. of Rome).

Lk. IV 10 (= Ps. XCI 11 τοῖς ἀγγέλοις αὐτοῦ ἐντελεῖται, cf. Acts XII 11, Apoc. XXII 16): Ael. Arist. 37, 7 (2, p. 15) the goddess Athena τῶν ἀγγέλων ἄλλοις ἄλλα ἐπιτάττει.

Lk. IV 36 (ἐν ἐξουσίᾳ καὶ δυνάμει, IX 1): Ael. Arist. 32, 14 (12, p. 139) ἐπ ἐξουσίας καὶ δυνάμεως.

Lk. V 21 (μόνος θεός, John V 44, XVII 3, Rom. XVI 27, 1 Tim. I 17, Jude 25): Ael. Arist. 37, 13 (2, p. 18) Ἀθηνᾶ ... μόνη. Cf. ibid. 26 (p. 26) and 2 (p. 13) παῖς ἐστι μόνη δὴ μόνου (sc. Athena of Zeus). On Zeus 43, 30 (1, p. 11) αὐτὸς μόνος, cf. 31 (p. 11). See G. Delling, ΜΟΝΟΣ ΘΕΟΣ, in *Studien zum Neuen Testament und zum hellenistischen Judentum*, Göttingen 1970, 391-400.

Lk. V 26 (εἴδομεν παράδοξα, sc. healings): Ael. Arist. 42, 8 (6, p. 67) καὶ μὴν τό γε παράδοξον πλεῖστον ἐν τοῖς ἰάμασι τοῦ θεοῦ (sc. of Asclepius). 48, 10 (24, p. 467) τῶν παραδόξων μνησθῆναι βούλομαι.

Lk. V 31 (par., Jesus as ἰατρός): Ael. Arist. 47, 4 (23, p. 446) παρέχειν ... ὥσπερ ἰατρῷ τῷ θεῷ. 47, 57 (23, p. 459) τὸν ἀληθινὸν καὶ προσήκοντα ἡμῖν ἰατρόν (sc. τὸν θεόν).

Lk. V 36-39 (par., opposition of παλαιός and καινός; cf. 2 Cor. V 17): Ael. Arist. 1, 355 (13, p. 306f.) μόνη δὴ πόλεων τὰ μὲν παλαιὰ τοῖς παλαιοῖς νικᾷ, τὰ δὲ καινὰ τοῖς καινοῖς, εἰ δὲ βούλει, τὰ μὲν παλαιὰ τοῖς καινοῖς, τὰ δὲ καινὰ τοῖς παλαιοῖς, τοῖς ἑαυτῆς λέγω τὰ τῶν ἄλλων (*schol. ad loc.* χιασμὸς τὸ σχῆμα).

Lk. VI 19 (ἰᾶσθαι said of Jesus, passim N.T., e.g. Acts IX 34): Ael. Arist. 43, 25 (1, p. 9) Ἀσκληπιὸς ἰᾶται.

Lk. VI 32-35 (cf. W. C. van Unnik, "Die Motivierung der Feindesliebe in Lukas VI 32-35", *Sparsa Collecta* I, Leiden 1973, 111-126): [Ael. Arist.] 54, p. 682 ὁ μὲν παρ' ὧν εὖ ἐπεπόνθει, τούτους οὐκ ἐθέλων τοῖς ἴσοις ἀμείψασθαι ἀγνωμοσύνης ἅμα καὶ ἀδικίας ἔγκλημα φέρεται.

Lk. VII 30 (βουλὴ τοῦ θεοῦ, Acts II 23, XIII 36, XX 27): Ael. Arist. 43, 25 (1, p. 9) Διὸς ... βουλήν.

Lk. VIII 11 ('seed' metaphorically used): Ael. Arist. 1, 45 (13, p. 170) ... ἵνα ... μὴ μόνον τῶν πυρῶν καὶ κριθῶν εἴη τὰ σπέρματα αὐτοῖς, ἀλλὰ καὶ δικαιοσύνης καὶ τῆς ἄλλης ἁπάσης διαίτης τε καὶ πολιτείας ἐκ θεῶν αὐτοῖς εἴη τὰ σπέρματα.

Lk. VIII 29 (Acts XVI 26, XX 23; only here, in Luke, the 'correct' Attic plural δεσμά is used, whereas in the rest of the N.T. δεσμοί is used): Ael. Arist. 46, 33 (3, p. 42) δεσμά (see Schmid, *Atticismus* II 17).

Lk. VIII 39 (διηγοῦ ὅσα σοι ἐποίησεν ὁ θεός, Acts XV 12 ἐξηγουμένων ὅσα ἐποίησεν ὁ θεὸς σημεῖα καὶ τέρατα, cf. II 11 and 1 Ptr. II 9): Ael. Arist. 40, 12 (5, p. 59) καταλέγειν ... δυνάμεις ἐμφανεῖς (of Heracles).

Lk. X 37 (positive valuation of ἔλεος, cf. James II 13): Ael. Arist. 11, 34 (33, p. 625) σύμφυτόν ἐστι τῇ πόλει ταύτῃ πάλαι τὸ παρὰ πᾶσιν εὐδοκιμοῦν ... ... ῥοπὴ πρὸς τοὺς ἀσθενεῖς καὶ ἔλεος τῶν ἀτυχούντων οὐ κενός, ἀλλὰ διαρκὴς εἰς σωτηρίαν.

Lk. XI 13 (ἀγαθὰ διδόναι): Ael. Arist. 46, 3 (3, p. 30) ἀγαθὰ διδόναι.

Lk. XI 27 (μακαρία ἡ κοιλία ἡ βαστάσασά σε): Ael. Arist. 30, 16 (10, p. 120) ἐξ οὗ τῆς μακαρίας προῆλθε γαστρός.

Lk. XI 49 (ἡ σοφία τοῦ θεοῦ, 1 Cor. I 21, 24, II 7, Eph. III 10): Ael. Arist. 36, 123 (48, p. 488) τῇ μεγάλῃ σοφίᾳ ... τοῦ θεοῦ.

Lk. XIII 16 (ἣν ἔδησεν ὁ σατανᾶς): Ael. Arist. 41, 7 (4, p. 49) δεδήσεται ... νόσῳ ... ὀργῇ ... τύχῃ.

Lk. XIV 26: Ael. Arist. 3, 252 (46, p. 258) οἱ δ' ἐπείθοντο, καὶ καταλιπόντες ἱερὰ καὶ τάφους καὶ γῆν εἰς ἕνα ἑώρων Θεμιστοκλέα, παίδων καὶ γονέων καὶ τῶν τῆς φύσεως ἀναγκαίων ἐκεῖνον προκρίναντες.

Lk. XV 12 (δός μοι τὸ ἐπιβάλλον μέρος): Ael. Arist. 1, 44 (13, p. 170) ... θεῶν ... διδόντων καὶ λαμβανόντων ἐκ τῶν αὐτῶν τὰ ἐπιβάλλοντα ἑκατέροις.

Lk. XVI 16 (πᾶς εἰς αὐτὴν βιάζεται): Ael. Arist. 1, 26 (13, p. 164) ... καὶ τοσοῦτον τῶν δημοποιήτων, οὓς αὐτοὶ ποιοῦνται, διαφέρουσιν, ὅσον οὐ κριθέντες ἄξιοι τῆς πολιτείας, ἀλλ' εἰσβιασάμενοι προὐβάλοντο τὴν πατρίδα.

Lk. XVIII 13 (Hebr. II 17, ἱλάσκεσθαι, but not with God as object, as in Ael. Arist.): Ael. Arist. 46, 3 (3, p. 30) ἐξιλάσασθαι ... τὸν θεόν.

Lk. XIX 43 (οἱ ἐχθροί σου ... συνέξουσίν σε (Jerusalem) πάντοθεν): Ael. Arist. 1, 235 (13, p. 263) ... οὕτω κοινῷ πολέμῳ βαρβάρων τε καὶ Ἑλλήνων συνεχομένην (sc. Athens).

Lk. XXI 11 (σεισμοί ..., φόβητρα ... ἀπ' οὐρανοῦ σημεῖα, 25 σημεῖα ἐν ἡλίῳ καὶ σελήνῃ καὶ ἄστροις, καὶ ἐπὶ τῆς γῆς συνοχὴ ἐθνῶν ἐν ἀπορίᾳ ἤχους θαλάσσης καὶ σάλου): Ael. Arist. 1, 116 (13, p. 206) ... διοσημίας (signs from Zeus) ... κυμάτων ἐπιρροήν, ... σκηπτούς, ... σεισμούς, ... νεφῶν ἢ χαλάζης ἐμβολήν, ... ἀήθεις ἀστέρας ... φόβους ἐγγείους ἢ θαλαττίους ... (*schol. ad loc.* ἅπαντες δὲ οὗτοι οὐκ ἀεὶ ὁρῶνται, ἀλλ' ὅταν φανῶσι, σημεῖα ἀνθρώποις δεινῶν μαντεύονται).

Lk. XXII 15 (ἐπιθυμίᾳ ἐπεθύμησα, Acts V 28 παραγγελίᾳ παρηγγείλαμεν, etc.; see Blass-Debrunner, par. 198): Ael. Arist. 3, 135 (46, p. 205) φυγῇ φευξούμεθα. This construction need not be a Semitism (a rendering of the Hebrew absolute infinitive as in the LXX).

Lk. XXII 25 (οἱ ἐξουσιάζοντες αὐτῶν εὐεργέται καλοῦνται): [Ael. Arist.] 54, p. 662 καὶ ὡς ἀληθῆ λέγω δῆλον ἐξ ὧν τοὺς μὲν τιμῶν ἀξιοῦμεν καὶ εὐεργέτας ἡμετέρους καὶ σωτῆρας καὶ πάντα τὰ τοιαῦτα καλοῦμεν.

Lk. XXIII 43 (2 Cor. XII 4, Apoc. II 7, παράδεισος as place of eternal bliss): Ael. Arist. 26, 99 (14, p. 365) ἡ γῆ πᾶσα οἷον παράδεισος (= garden, park) συγκεκόσμηται.

Lk. XXIV 1 (ὄρθρου βαθέως, only *h.l.*): Ael. Arist. 51, 42 (27, p. 544) ἐξ ὄρθρου βαθέος.

Lk. XXIV 7 (proleptic construction, also in John V 42, VIII 54): Ael. Arist. 40, 10 (5, p. 57) ἴσμεν Αἰγυπτίους ὅσον τινὰ ἄγουσιν θεὸν Ἡρακλέα καὶ Τυρίους ὅτι πρῶτον σέβουσι θεῶν.

Lk. XXIV 19 (λόγῳ καὶ ἔργῳ/ἔργῳ καὶ λόγῳ/λόγοις καὶ ἔργοις, Acts VII 22, Rom. XV 18, 2 Cor. X 11, Col. III 17, 2 Thess. II 17, 1 John III 18): Ael. Arist. 47, 16 (23, p. 449) ἐκεῖ λόγῳ τις ἠγωνίζετο, ἔργῳ δὲ οὔ. 2, 279 (45, p. 87) καὶ λόγῳ καὶ ἔργω σύμψηφον ὄντα αὐτόν μοι δείξω. 26, 34 (14, p. 336) λόγῳ καὶ ἔργω. Cf. 1, 99 (13, p. 198), 32, 23 (12, p. 142), 10, 43 (39, p. 750), etc.

JOHN

John I 1 (1 John I 1, II 13f.): Ael. Arist. 43, 8 and 9 (1, p. 3) οὐδ' ἔστι πρεσβύτερον οὐδὲν Διός, ... ἦν ... ἐξ ἀρχῆς.

John I 3 (τὰ πάντα = the universe): Ael. Arist. 43, 13 (1, p. 5) τετάρτῳ τούτῳ (sc. πυρί) τὰ πάντα κατέλαβε. Cf. 43, 9 (1, p. 3).

John I 4 (τὸ φῶς τῶν ἀνθρώπων, cf. v. 9 et passim): Ael. Arist. 45, 33 (8, p. 97) ὦ κοινὸν ἅπασιν ἀνθρώποις φῶς (= Sarapis). 35, 38 (9, p. 112) ὦ φῶς τῆς ἀνθρωπίνης εὐδαιμονίας (= the emperor).

John I 9 (τὸ φῶς τὸ αληθινόν, 1 John II 8): Ael. Arist. 23, 15 (42, p. 772) τοῦ θεοῦ ... ἀληθινὸν φῶς ἀνίσχοντος.

John I 14 (ἐσκήνωσεν ἐν ἡμῖν): Ael. Arist. 38, 22 (7, p. 79) οὐδ' ὑμῖν (sc. the Asclepiads) θᾶκοι χωρὶς ἀλλήλων οὐδὲ διεσκηνήσατε.

John I 18 (ὁ ὢν εἰς τὸν κόλπον τοῦ πατρός, cf. Hebr. X 12 εἰς τὸ διηνεκὲς ἐκάθισεν ἐν δεξιᾷ τοῦ θεοῦ): Ael. Arist. 37, 4 (2, p. 13f.) the goddess Athena αἰεὶ πάρεστί τε καὶ συνδιαιτᾶται (sc. Διί) ... καὶ σύνεστι μόνη μόνῳ.

John I 18 (μονογενής, cf. v. 14, III 16.18, 1 John IV 9): Ael. Arist. 37, 2 (2, p. 13) τοῦ πάντων δημιουργοῦ ... παῖς ἐστι μόνη μόνου. ... ἐστὶ μόνη βεβαίως γνησία τοῦ πατρός (sc. the goddess Athena).

John I 18 (ἐξηγήσατο): Ael. Arist. 37, 7 (2, p. 15) ... ἀντ' ἐξηγητοῦ τινος οὖσα τοῖς θεοῖς (sc. the goddess Athena). 1, 62 (13, p. 181) τὸν κοινὸν τῶν Ἑλλήνων ἐξηγητήν, ..., τὸν Απόλλω τὸν Πύθιον.

John II 11 (ταύτην ἐποίησεν ἀρχὴν τῶν σημείων): Ael. Arist. 48, 50 (24, p. 478) καὶ πρῶτον ἦν τῶν θαυμάτων τοῦτο.

John IV 10 (τὴν δωρεὰν τοῦ θεοῦ, cf. Acts VIII 20, Eph. II 8, Hebr. XI): 4 Ael. Arist. 43, 6 (1, p. 2) τῶν Διὸς ... δωρεῶν. 45, 16 (8, p. 88) τὰ ... τῶν θεῶν ... δῶρα.

John IV 14 (πηγή metaphorically used, cf. Apoc. VII 17, XXI 6): Ael. Arist. 40, 17 (5, p. 61) ἀρετῆς ὡσπερεὶ πηγή.

John IV 34 (πέμπειν used of God who sends Jesus, passim, especially in the Gospel of John): Ael. Arist. 43, 20 (1, p. 8) Zeus ἔπεμπεν εἰς ἀνθρώπους Αἰδῶ καὶ Δίκην.

John V 1ff.: Ael. Arist. 39, 14-15 (18, p. 412-3) (on the healing power of the well of Asclepius) ἀλλὰ καὶ τἄλλα ὁ θεὸς αὐτῷ (sc. τῷ φρέατι) χρῆται ὥσπερ ἄλλῳ τῷ συνεργῷ, καὶ πολλοῖς ἤδη πολλάκις τὸ φρέαρ τοῦτο συνεβάλετο εἰς τὸ τυχεῖν ὧν ἔχρῃζον παρὰ τοῦ θεοῦ. ὥσπερ γὰρ οἱ παῖδες οἱ τῶν ἰατρῶν τε καὶ θαυματοποιῶν γεγυμνασμένοι πρὸς τὰς διακονίας εἰσὶ καὶ συμπράττοντες ἐκπλήττουσι τοὺς θεωμένους καὶ χρωμένους, οὕτω τοῦ μεγάλου θαυματοποιοῦ καὶ πάντα ἐπὶ σωτηρίᾳ πράττοντος ἀνθρώπων εὕρημα τοῦτο καὶ κτῆμά ἐστι· συμπράττει δὴ πρὸς ἅπαντα αὐτῷ καὶ γίγνεται πολλοῖς ἀντὶ φαρμάκου. πολλοὶ μὲν γὰρ τούτῳ λουσάμενοι ὀφθαλμοὺς ἐκομίσαντο, πολλοὶ δὲ πιόντες στέρνον ἰάθησαν καὶ τὸ ἀναγκαῖον πνεῦμα ἀπέλαβον, τῶν δὲ πόδας ἐξώρθωσεν, τῶν δὲ ἄλλο τι· ἤδη δέ τις πιὼν ἐξ ἀφώνου φωνὴν ἀφῆκεν, ὥσπερ οἱ τῶν ἀπορρήτων ὑδάτων πιόντες μαντικοὶ γιγνόμενοι· τοῖς δὲ καὶ αὐτὸ τὸ ἀρύτεσθαι ἀντ' ἄλλης σωτηρίας καθέστηκεν. καὶ τοῖς τε δὴ νοσοῦσιν οὕτως ἀλεξιφάρμακον καὶ σωτήριόν ἐστιν καὶ τοῖς ὑγιαίνουσιν ἐνδιαιτωμένοις παντὸς ἄλλου χρῆσιν ὕδατος οὐκ ἄμεμπτον ποιεῖ. (See Rengstorf, *Anfänge der Auseinandersetzung* ... 19ff.). Cf. 11 (p. 411) διάκονόν τε καὶ συνεργὸν τοῦ φιλανθρωποτάτου τῶν θεῶν (sc. τὸ φρέαρ τοῦ Ἀσκληπιοῦ). ... οὔτε ἐκεῖνος ἄγει σχολὴν ἄλλο τι πράττειν ἢ σῴζειν ἀνθρώπους καὶ τοῦτο μιμούμενον τὸν δεσπότην αἰεὶ πληροῖ τὴν τῶν δεομένων χρείαν. Cf. also 47, 18 (23, p. 449) ἔπειτα ἐδόκει μοι παραθαρρύνειν Φοῖβος παρών, ὥστε καὶ εἰς τὸ ὕδωρ εἰσέβαινον ἀνυπόπτως ἤδη.

John V 17 (ἐργάζεσθαι of God, Acts XIII 41): Ael. Arist. 40, 12 (5, p. 59) θαυμαστὰ οἷα ἐργάζεται (sc. Heracles).

John V 23 (to honour God, 1 Tim. I 17, etc.): Ael. Arist. 23, 25 (42, p. 776) τὴν τῆς θεοῦ τιμήν. 24, 48 (44, p. 840) τιμᾶν μὲν τοὺς θεούς. 45, 5 (8, p. 84) πάντας οὖν καὶ τιμᾶν αὐτοὺς (sc. the gods) εἰκὸς ἀπὸ τῆς ὑπαρχούσης ἑκάστοις δυνάμεως.

John V 39 (the Scriptures are μαρτυροῦσαι, Rom. III 21): Ael. Arist. 24, 46 (44, p. 839) ... τὰ ὑπὸ τῶν ποιητῶν εἰς ὑμᾶς εἰρημένα, ὧν ἐγὼ τοὺς λόγους ὑπερβὰς τῆς Ὁμήρου μόνης μαρτυρίας μνησθήσομαι.

John VI 28f. (τὰ ἔργα τοῦ θεοῦ, passim): Ael. Arist. 43, 6 (1, p. 2) τὰ Διὸς ἔργα. 37, 9 (2, p. 16) τὸ ἔργον αὐτῆς (sc. Ἀθηνᾶς). 45, 16 (8, p. 88) τίνα οὖν ἔργα Σαράπιδος; ... τὰ τοῦ μεγίστου τῶν θεῶν ἔργα. Cf. 23, 19 (42, p. 774).

John VIII 36 (ἐλευθεροῦν, said of Christ; Gal. V 1): Ael. Arist. 40, 5 (5, p. 54) (on Heracles) ... αὐτῷ προσῆκον ἐλευθεροῦν.

John IX 4 (X 25.32.37): Ael. Arist. 37, 28 (2, p. 27) ἔξεστιν τὰ τοῦ Διὸς ἔργα κοινὰ τοῦ Διὸς εἶναι φῆσαι καὶ τῆς Ἀθηνᾶς.

John IX 7: Ael. Arist. 48, 18 (24, p. 470) Asclepius κελεύει καταβάντα εἰς τὸν ποταμὸν τὸν πρὸ τῆς πόλεως ῥέοντα λούσασθαι.

John X 11ff. ('shepherd' metaphorically used, Hebr. XIII 20, 1 Ptr. II 25): [Ael. Arist.] 35, 22 (9, p. 106) ὁ βασιλεὺς ἡμερότητι καὶ ἐπιεικείᾳ διενήνοχεν ... ὥστε μικρὸν ... ποιμὴν τῶν λαῶν εἰπεῖν εἶναι.

John X 18 (λαμβάνειν παρὰ τοῦ πατρός, Acts II 33, Apoc. II 28): Ael. Arist. 37, 7 (2, p. 15) παρὰ τοῦ πατρὸς παραλαμβάνουσα (Ἀθηνᾶ).

John XI 50 (Christ dies for others, XVIII 14, Rom. V 6-8, XIV 15, 1 Cor. XV 3, 2 Cor. V 15, 1 Thess. V 10, 1 Ptr. III 18, cf. Mk. X 45): Ael. Arist. 48, 44 (24, p. 476) οὐ μέντοι πρότερόν γε ὁ πυρετὸς παντελῶς ἐξέλιπεν, πρὶν ἐτελεύτησέ μοι τῶν τροφίμων ὁ πλείστου ἄξιος. τῇ δ' αὐτῇ ἡμέρᾳ, ὡς ὕστερον ἔγνων, ἐκεῖνός τε ἐτεθνήκει καὶ ἡ νόσος ᾤχετο ἀπιοῦσα. οὕτω τόν τε ἄχρι τούτου χρόνον δωρεὰν ἔσχον παρὰ τῶν θεῶν καὶ μετὰ τοῦτο ἀνεβίων ὑπὸ τοῖς θεοῖς, καί τις οἷον ἀντίδοσις αὕτη συνέβη. Cf. 1, 87 (13, p. 192) (λέγεται) Κόδρος ἐν τῷ πρὸς Δωριέας πολέμῳ καὶ Πελοποννησίους αὐτὸς ἐθελοντὴς ὑπὲρ τῆς χώρας ἀποθανεῖν. *ibid.* (p. 191), λέγεται γὰρ Ἐρεχθεὺς ... τὴν θυγατέρα ὑπὲρ τῆς πόλεως ἐπιδοῦναι, τοῦ θεοῦ χρήσαντος, ...

John XIV 16 (?): Ael. Arist. 1, 51 (13, p. 174) Heracles διατελεῖ δὴ θεὸς ὤν. 40, 16 (5, p. 60) τὰ μὲν, ἡνίκ' ἐν ἀνθρώποις ἦν (sc. Heracles), τὰ δὲ καὶ νῦν ἔτι φαίνεται πράττων αὐτὸς ἐφ' ἑαυτοῦ.

John XV 5 (χωρὶς ἐμοῦ οὐ δύνασθε ποιεῖν οὐδέν): Ael. Arist. 37, 10 (2, p. 16) οὐδ' αὖ πράξουσί ποτε χρηστὸν οὐδὲν ἄνευ τῆς Ἀθηνᾶς. 50, 102 (26, p. 531) ἔφην γὰρ ὡς οὐδὲν οὔτε μεῖζον ἔλαττον οἷόν τ' εἴη πράττειν μοι ἄνευ τοῦ θεοῦ.

John XVI 7 (ἀπέρχομαι): Ael. Arist. 1, 50 (13, p. 173) Ἡρακλέους ἀπελθόντος ἐξ ἀνθρώπων ἡ μὲν πόλις καὶ νεὼς καὶ βωμοὺς ἱδρύεται πρώτη. Cf. 40, 11 (5, p. 58) ἀπῆλθεν ἐξ ἀνθρώπων Ἡρακλῆς.

John XVI 30 (οἶδας πάντα, cf. XVIII 4): Ael. Arist. 43, 6 (1, p. 2) (Μοῦσαι) πάντ' εἰδυῖαι.

John XVII 11 and 22 (ἵνα ὦσιν ἓν καθὼς ἡμεῖς ἕν): Ael. Arist. 37, 27 (2, p. 27) αἰεὶ ταὐτὸν ἀμφοῖν (Zeus and Athena) δοκεῖ.

John XXI 24: Ael. Arist. 45, 31 (8, p. 96) καὶ ἡμῖν ἤδη προειρήσθω κοινῷ λόγῳ ὥσπερ ἐν σπονδῶν ἀπαγγελίᾳ· πάντως οὐ δέος μὴ ψευσώμεθα.

John XXI 25 (cf. XX 31): Ael. Arist. 1, 230 (13, p. 260) οὐ συγγραφῆς ἔργον ψιλῆς προειλόμεθα ἀφηγεῖσθαι τὰ πεπραγμένα τῇ πόλει, καὶ γὰρ ἂν εἰς τὴν ἐπιοῦσαν πεντετηρίδα ἐκτείνοιτο ὁ λόγος, ἀλλὰ τῶν μὲν κατὰ τοὺς πολέμους πράξεων τὰς γνωριμωτάτας εἰπεῖν, τῶν δ' ὑπαρχόντων ἀγαθῶν τῇ πόλει καθ' ὅσον δυνατὸν μηδὲν παραλιπεῖν. 45, 30 (8, p. 95) ἐμοὶ δ' ἐγχειροῦντι λέγειν (sc. all the deeds of Sarapis) ἡμερῶν πλῆθος ἐπιρρυὲν ἀτέλεστον ὁμοίως ἕξει τὸν κατάλογον. 47, 2 23, p. 445) ὅσοι πώποτε τῶν φίλων ἐδεήθησαν ἢ προὔτρεψαν εἰπεῖν καὶ συγγράψαι περὶ αὐτῶν (sc. τῶν τοῦ Σωτῆρος ἀγωνισμάτων), οὐδενὶ πώποτε ἐπείσθην, φεύγων τὸ ἀδύνατον. ἐδόκει γάρ μοι παραπλήσιον εἶναι ὥσπερ ἂν εἰ διὰ παντὸς τοῦ πελάγους ὕφαλος διεξελθὼν εἶτ' ἠναγκαζόμην ἀποδιδόναι λόγον, πόσοις τισὶ τοῖς πᾶσιν ῥοθίοις ἐνέτυχον. *ibid.* 49 (p. 457) τοιαῦτ' ἅττα ἠμειψάμην αὐτούς. ἦν δὲ μυρία ἄλλα καὶ γιγνόμενα καὶ λεγόμενα, κρείττω λόγου τε καὶ ἐλπίδος.

ACTS

Acts I 1ff. (Jesus first lived among the people, but now lives with God and is God): Ael. Arist. 1, 374 (13, p. 311) ἀλλὰ μὴν Ἡρακλέα γε καὶ Διοσκούρους ἅπαντες δήπου θεοὺς εἶναι νομίζουσι· τούτοις δέ γε, ἕως ὡμίλουν ἀνθρώποις, πρώτοις ξένων ἡ πόλις δείκνυσι τὰ ἱερά.

Acts I 8 (ἕως ἐσχάτου τῆς γῆς, XIII 47): Ael. Arist. 2, 40 (45, p. 12) ἐπ' ἔσχατα τῆς γῆς. 35, 14 (9, p. 103) πρὸς ἔσχατα γῆς. 1, 117 (13, p. 206) εἰς ἔσχατα γῆς. *ibid.* 119 (p. 208); 25, 40 (43, p. 812); 40, 18 (5, p. 56); 26, 70 (14, p. 350) ἐπ' ἐσχατιαῖς (γῆς). In the last-mentioned passage the expression is clarified by Γετῶν . . . Λιβύων . . . τῶν περὶ τὴν ἐρυθρὰν θάλατταν.

Acts I 16 (προεῖπεν τὸ πνεῦμα τὸ ἅγιον διὰ στόματος Δαυίδ): Ael. Arist. 3, 250 (46, p. 257) θεῶν τις διὰ τῆς Θεμιστοκλέους γλώττης ἐφθέγξατο.

Acts II 1-13 (1 Cor. XII 10, 28-30): Ael. Arist. 28, 114-115 (49, p. 528) is a long description of speaking under divine inspiration.

Acts II 3-4: Ael. Arist. 28, 110 (49, p. 527) λόγων δ' αὕτη πηγὴ μία, τὸ ὡς ἀληθῶς ἱερὸν καὶ θεῖον πῦρ τὸ ἐκ Διὸς ἑστίας.

Acts II 4: Ael. Arist. 2, 53 (45, p. 17) (on inspiration) μανία τίς ἐστιν ἀμείνων σωφροσύνης καὶ παρὰ θεῶν ἀνθρώποις γιγνομένη.

Acts II 11 (λαλούντων . . . τὰ μεγαλεῖα τοῦ θεοῦ, XIV 27b, 1 Ptr. II 9): Ael. Arist. 37, 27 (2, p. 27) εἰπεῖν εἰς τὸ μέσον τὰ τῆς θεοῦ. 43, 6 (1, p. 2) εἰπεῖν περὶ Διός.

Acts II 21 (et passim, ἐπικαλεῖσθαι of God): Ael. Arist. 47, 17 (23, p. 449) προσευχομένου δέ μου καὶ ἀνακαλοῦντος τὸν θεόν . . .

Acts II 29 (εἰπεῖν μετὰ παρρησίας, IV 29, 31, XXVIII 31): Ael. Arist. 6, 2 (30, p. 571) ἀξιῶ δὲ γενέσθαι μοι μετὰ παρρησίας εἰπεῖν. See *ad* IV 29.

Acts II 31 (οὔτε ἐγκατελείφθη εἰς ᾅδην): Ael. Arist. 37, 25 (2, p. 25) καὶ τοῦτο μὲν εἰς Ἅιδου ζῶντα (sc. Heracles) κομίσασα ζῶντα ἐξήγαγε (sc. Athena), κρατήσαντα τοῦ Κερβέρου.

Acts II 31 (Gal. III 8, on the προορᾶν of the Scriptures): Ael. Arist. 26, 106 (14, p. 368) δοκεῖ δέ μοι καὶ Ἡσίοδος, εἰ ὁμοίως Ὁμήρῳ τέλειος ἦν τὰ ποιητικὰ καὶ μαντικός, ὥσπερ ἐκεῖνος οὐκ ἠγνόησεν τὴν ὑμετέραν ἀρχὴν ἐσομένην, ἀλλὰ προεῖδεν καὶ ἀνεφθέγξατο ἐν τοῖς ἔπεσιν, οὕτως καὶ αὐτὸς ...

Acts II 44: Ael. Arist. 27, 24 (16, p. 392) on M. Antoninus and L. Verus, οὗτοι γάρ εἰσιν οἱ τὴν παροιμίαν ἐπὶ πλεῖστον ἄραντες καὶ διὰ τῶν μεγίστων ἔργων ὅρον δείξαντες ὅτι τῷ ὄντι κοινὰ τὰ φίλων. 24, 42 (44, p. 837) τὸ λεγόμενον δὴ τοῦτο πάντα κοινά.

Acts II 46f. (καθ' ἡμέραν ... αἰνοῦντες τὸν θεόν): Ael. Arist. 40, 1 (5, p. 53) μέγιστον δὲ ὁ καθ' ἡμέραν ὑπὸ πάντων ἔπαινος ἐπὶ πάσης τῆς παραπιπτούσης προφάσεως αἰεὶ γιγνόμενος.

Acts III 13 (Jesus as παῖς θεοῦ, III 26, IV 25.27.30): Ael. Arist. 37, 2 (2, p. 13) the goddess Athena τοῦ πάντων δημιουργοῦ καὶ βασιλέως παῖς ἐστι. 40, 22 (5, p. 62) Heracles as Διὸς παῖς. 42, 4 (6, p. 65) Asclepius as Ἀπόλλωνος παῖδα.

Acts III 15 (Jesus as ἀρχηγός, V 31, Hebr. II 10, XII 2): Ael. Arist. 43, 8 (1, p. 3) Zeus is ἀρχηγέτης τῶν πάντων. Cf. 30, 1 (10, p. 113) Asclepius as τοῦ βίου καθηγεμών.

Acts IV 29 (δὸς τοῖς δούλοις σου μετὰ παρρησίας πάσης λαλεῖν, cf. Eph. VI 19f.): Ael. Arist. 23, 61 (42, p. 788) καί μοι πρὸς Διὸς δοθήτω τι παρρησίας ἤδη.

Acts IV 30 (God is asked τὴν χεῖρα ἐκτείνειν): Ael. Arist. 42, 10 (6, p. 68) ὁ θεὸς χεῖρα ὤρεξεν. See also *ad* Lk. I 66.

Acts V 29 (and 32, πειθαρχεῖν θεῷ, cf. ὑπακούω passim, e.g. Hebr. V 9): Ael. Arist. 51, 56 (27, p. 548) πάντα λῆρος πρὸς τὸ πείθεσθαι τῷ θεῷ. Cf. 43, 25 (1, p. 10). 47, 63 (23, p. 461) καὶ δηλαδὴ οὐχ αἵρεσις ἦν ἢ τῶν ἰατρῶν ἀκούειν ἢ τοῦ θεοῦ. 49, 9 (25, p. 490) ταῦτα συνεβούλευε, κἀγὼ τὸ μὲν τοῦ αἵματος οὐκ ἔφην εἶναι κύριος οὔτε οὕτως οὔτ' ἐκείνως ποιεῖν, ἀλλ' ἕως ἂν ὁ θεὸς προστάττῃ ἀφαιρεῖν, ὑπακούσεσθαι καὶ ἑκὼν καὶ ἄκων, μᾶλλον δὲ οὐδέποτε ἄκων.

Acts V 29 (Πέτρος καὶ οἱ ἀπόστολοι, XVII 25 διδοὺς πᾶσι ζωὴν καὶ πνοὴν καὶ τὰ πάντα. The following passages from Ael. Arist. illustrate this use of καί in the sense of "and generally; and other..." See on this use the observations by W. J. Verdenius in *Mnemosyne* 1954, 38; 1956, 250; 1974, 21. τε may have the same function, also in εἴτε; see e.g. in the N.T. 1 Cor. X 31 εἴτε οὖν ἐσθίετε εἴτε πίνετε εἴτε τι ποιεῖτε): Ael. Arist. 28, 72 (49, p. 515) ὦ Ζεῦ καὶ θεοί. 25, 69 (43, p. 823) Ζεῦ καὶ πάντες θεοί. 9, 32 (38, p. 723) ὦ Ζεῦ καὶ Πόσειδον καὶ πάντες θεοί. 9, 46 (38, p. 730) τῷ Διὶ τῷ ἐλευθερίῳ καὶ Ἡρακλεῖ τῷ ἀλεξικάκῳ καὶ Ἀπόλλωνι τῷ Πυθίῳ καὶ Ἰσμηνίῳ καὶ θεοῖς καὶ ἥρωσι. 2, 53 (45, p. 17) ὦ Ζεῦ καὶ θεοί. 2, 34 (45, p. 11) Πλάτων καὶ ἅπαντες λέγουσιν ... 33, 20 (51, p. 577) παῖδας καὶ γονέας καὶ πράξεις τε καὶ ἀναπαύσεις καὶ πάντα. 1, 326 (13, p. 295) ὦ Λακεδαιμόνιοι καὶ πάντες Ἕλληνες. 1, 321 (13, p. 293) εἰς αὐτὴν (sc. the city of Athens) καὶ εἰς τοὺς Ἕλληνας. 45, 20 (8, p. 90) ἐν πανηγύρεσί τε καὶ πάσαις ἡμέραις. 22, 3 (19, p. 416) ποιηταὶ καὶ λογοποιοὶ καὶ συγγραφεῖς πάντες.

Acts V 36 (διελύθησαν καὶ ἐγένοντο εἰς οὐδέν): Ael. Arist. 1, 84 (13, p. 190) καὶ διελέλυτο Ἀμαζόσιν ἥ τε ἀρχὴ καὶ ὁ δρόμος (after having been defeated by the Athenians).

Acts VII 10 (χάριν διδόναι, Rom. XII 3.6, XV 15, 1 Cor. I 4, III 10, Gal. II 9, Eph. III 8, IV 7.29, Jas. IV 6): Ael. Arist. 37, 1 (2, p. 12) σὺ δ', ... Ἀθηνᾶ, ... δίδου ... χάριν. Cf. 1, 404 (13, p. 320).

Acts VII 22 (πάσῃ σοφίᾳ Αἰγυπτίων): Ael. Arist. 2, 169 (45, p. 52) τὴν δ' Αἰγυπτίων σοφίαν τίς οὐκ οἶδεν τῶν ἐντετυχηκότων; 3, 180 (46, p. 225) Αἰγύπτιοι δὲ οἱ σοφώτατοι πάντων. 26, 73 (14, p. 351) ... ὥσπερ καὶ ἄλλα πολλὰ παρὰ τοὺς ἄλλους ἐδόκουν εἶναι, ᾗ φασιν, Αἰγύπτιοι σοφοί.

Acts VII 31 (XII 22, φωνὴ θεοῦ): Ael. Arist. 40, 22 (5, p. 62) φωνῆς θείας.

Acts VII 38 (λόγια = the words of God, cf. Rom. III 2, Hebr. V 12, 1 Ptr. IV 11): Ael. Arist. 1, 173 (13, p. 233) τῶν ἐκ Δελφῶν λογίων ... διαρρήδην μαρτυρούντων. 48, 36 (24, p. 474) πολλὰ ἄλλα λόγια ... ἐδηλώθη.

Acts VII 55f.: Ael. Arist. 50, 56 (26, p. 519) ἀνασχὼν τὴν χεῖρα δείκνυσί μου τόπον τινὰ τοῦ οὐρανοῦ, ... ἀναβλέπω τε δὴ καὶ ὁρῶ Ἀσκληπιὸν τὸν ἐν Περγάμῳ ἐνιδρυμένον ἐν τῷ οὐρανῷ. Cf. 48, 41 (24, p. 475f.).

Acts VIII 5 (κηρύσσειν Ἰησοῦν/Χριστόν, IX 20, XIX 13, 1 Cor. I 23, etc.): Ael. Arist. 45, 20 (8, p. 90) πῶς οὖν οὐ τοῦτον (sc. Sarapis) ἀνακηρύττειν χρὴ ...; For χρή cf. 1 Cor. IX 16.

Acts VIII 36 (τί κωλύει): Ael. Arist. 2, 49 (45, p. 14) τί κωλύει καὶ ῥητορικὴν τῆς Ἑρμοῦ τιθέναι δωρεᾶς; 2, 148 (45, p. 46) τί κωλύει καὶ ῥητορικὴν τέχνην εἶναι ...; 2, 271 (45, p. 84) τί κωλύει καὶ τοὺς νόμους αὐτὸν ἅπαντας ... διαγράφειν; 2, 358 (45, p. 119) τί κωλύει καὶ ἡμᾶς ... ἀντιθεῖναι; 16, 35 (52, p. 605) τί κωλύει καὶ ἡμᾶς αὔριον κεῖσθαι τηνικάδε ὁμοῦ τοῖς ἄλλοις ἀναμεμιγμένους; 3, 133 (46, p. 204) εἴ γε τὴν ἀρχὴν δουλείαν εἶναι τιθείημεν, τί κωλύει καὶ τὴν δουλείαν ἀρχὴν τοῖς αὐτοῖς τούτοις τιθέναι λόγοις; 12, 18 (34, p. 649) τί κωλύει τοὺς ὑπάρχοντας τοῦ κακουργεῖν ὡς γενναίους θαυμάζειν; 13, 20 (35, p. 678) εἰ ταῦθ' οὕτω φαίνεται, τί κωλύει Λακεδαιμονίους ὁμοῦ σῴζειν καὶ τὴν πόλιν δι' ἀσφαλείας ποιεῖσθαι; 2, 361 (45, p. 120) τί κωλύει μηδ' Ἀριστείδην ... ἔξω τῆς ἐκείνων αἰτίας τιθέναι; 2, 412 (45, p. 140) τί κωλύει προθεραπεύειν τὰ πολλὰ τῇ ῥητορικῇ ...; 2, 446 (45, p. 150) τί κωλύει ... ἡμᾶς ... ὀρθῶς ποιεῖν; Cf. further 34, 8 (50, p. 548); 3, 214 (46, p. 240), 3, 265 (46, p. 263); 3, 411 (46, p. 316); 3, 454 (46, p. 329); 3, 593 (46, p. 375); 2, 449 (45, p. 151), and many other instances. This material casts doubt upon O. Cullmann's interpretation of Acts VIII 36 ("eine alte Taufformel") in his *Die Tauflehre des N.T.*, Zürich 1948, 65ff.

Acts IX 1 (ἐμπνέων ἀπειλῆς καὶ φόνου. On this use of πνέω and compounds see P. W. van der Horst in *Novum Testamentum* 12 (1970), 257-269): Ael. Arist. 15, 16 (37, p. 700) δῆλον δὲ καὶ χωρὶς τῶν παρὰ τούτων λόγων ὅτι πάντα τὸν ἔμπροσθεν χρόνον συμπνέοντες καὶ κοινωνοῦντες ἑκάστων, ..., οὐδὲν περὶ ὑμῶν ἁπλοῦν οὐδὲ δίκαιον φρονήσουσιν ὕστερον.

Acts IX 3 (light as a divine manifestation, cf. XII 7, XXII 6.9, XXVI 13): Ael. Arist. 38, 23 (7, p. 79) (said to the Asclepiads) αἰεὶ δ', ὥσπερ ἀνθρώπῳ σκιά, φῶς ὅποι κινοῖσθε ἕπεται. 51, 64 (27, p. 550) ἐπιστρέψαντος δέ μου ὡς πρὸς τὴν ἀκρόπολιν, ἵν' οἴκαδε εἰσέλθοιμι, διῇξεν σέλας ἐκ δεξιᾶς καὶ κατέσκηψεν οὕτω δή τι παρ' αὐτὰς ἄκρας μου τὰς κόμας ὥστε ἐθαύμαζον εἰ μὴ ἡμμέναι εἶεν.

Acts IX 4 (XXII 7, XXVI 14, 2 Cor. XII 4, Apoc. I 10): Ael. Arist. 48, 41 (24, p. 476) τῶν λόγων ... ὧν ἤκουσα παρὰ τῆς θεοῦ.

Acts IX 10-12 (the motif of the double-dream or double-vision, cf. X 4ff.10ff.): Ael. Arist. 47, 66 (23, p. 462) ὁ Σωτὴρ σημαίνει τῆς αὐτῆς νυκτὸς ταὐτὸν ἐμοί τε καὶ τῷ τροφεῖ ..., ὥστε ἐγὼ μὲν ἔπεμπον ἐκείνῳ φράσων ἃ εἰρηκὼς εἴη ὁ θεός, ὁ δ' ἀπήντα φράσων αὐτός μοι ἃ ἠκηκόει τοῦ θεοῦ. 48, 30 (24, p. 473) τούτῳ γίγνεται τῆς αὐτῆς νυκτὸς ὄψις ὀνείρατος ἥπερ κἀμοί, μικρὰ δέ πως παρήλλαττεν. 48, 48 (24, p. 477) καί τινι τῶν ἐκ τῆς Ῥωμαίων βουλῆς παρεδρεύοντι καὶ αὐτῷ ταὐτὸν τοῦτο ἐκέλευσεν (sc. ὁ θεός), ἐπισημηνάμενος ὅτι καὶ Ἀριστείδῃ προστέτακται. See Wikenhauser, Doppelträume (see Bibl.).

Acts IX 34 (ἰᾶταί σε Ἰησοῦς Χριστός, et al.): Ael. Arist. 47, 67 (23, p. 462) ... ὃ λάθρα ἰᾶτο (sc. ὁ θεός). 49, 12 (25, p. 491) an oracle says Ἰήσεταί σε νοῦσον ἠδ' ἀκέσσεται Ἀσκληπιός.

Acts IX 38 (μὴ ὀκνήσῃς διελθεῖν ἕως ἡμῶν): Ael. Arist. 46, 2 (3, p. 29) ἔγνων μὴ ὀκνητέον εἶναί μοι διὰ ταῦτα παρελθεῖν εἰς ὑμᾶς.

Acts X 9ff.: Ael. Arist. 47, 50 (23, p. 458) Aristides acts on the basis of a symbolical interpretation of a dream: ἥμεσα εἰς ἑσπέραν, ἐνθύμιον ποιησάμενος τὸ τοῦ χοῦ τοῦ ἐκφορουμένου. 48, 2 (24, p. 465) ὄψεις ὀνειράτων ἀναγκάζουσιν ἡμᾶς κτλ. Cf. also 50, 101 (26, p. 531).

Acts X 14 (μηδαμῶς, κύριε, cf. XI 8): Ael. Arist. 5, 46 (29, p. 569) ὑμεῖς δὲ ... προκαταγνώσεσθε μηδὲν ἔτ' εἶναι τῶν ἐκεῖ κατασχεῖν· μηδαμῶς. 8, 16 (32, p. 606) εἶτα τούτοις ἡμεῖς ὀργιζόμεθα; μηδαμῶς. Cf. 11, 50 (33, p. 632) and 9, 43f. (38, p. 728).

Acts X 28 (ὁ θεὸς ἔδειξεν κτλ.): Ael. Arist. 47, 52 (23, p. 458) ἔξοδον προὔδειξεν ὁ θεός.

Acts X 33 (God προστάσσει in a dream, cf. Mt. I 24): Ael. Arist. 51, 17 (27, p. 538) in a dream God προσέταξεν ἀναστρέφειν. ... αὐθημερὸν ἐξιέναι ἐπὶ τῷ προστάγματι (sc. τοῦ θεοῦ). 49, 20 (25, p. 493) καί μοι γίγνεται πρόσταγμα, sc. of God in a dream. Cf. 50, 14 (26, p. 505).

Acts X 38 (Jesus διῆλθεν εὐεργετῶν καὶ ἰώμενος πάντας): Ael. Arist. 40, 4 (5, p. 54) (on Heracles) πάντας ἐφεξῆς ἐπιών, τούς τε ἐν ταῖς νήσοις καὶ τοὺς κατ' ἤπειρον, οὐδὲν τῶν εἰς εὐεργεσίαν φερόντων ἐλλείπων. 37, 10 (2, p. 16) ὅσας εὐεργεσίας κατέθετο, sc. Athena. 38, 19 (7, p. 77f.) (on the Asclepiads) οἱ δὲ ἕως μὲν ἦσαν ἐν ἀνθρώποις, ... τὰς πόλεις ὠφέλουν, οὐ μόνον τὰς τοῦ σώματος νόσους ἐξαιροῦντες, ἀλλὰ καὶ τὰ τῶν πόλεων νοσήματα ἰώμενοι. 38, 14 (7, p. 75) the Asclepiads ὥσπερεὶ κεφάλαιον τοῦτο ἐπέθηκαν τῶν εἰς τοὺς Ἕλληνας εὐεργεσιῶν, προσθήσω δὲ καὶ εἰς ἅπαντας ἤδη, κτλ. 43, 25 (1, p. 10) Hera and Artemis εὐεργετοῦσιν ἀνθρώπους. 42, 5 (6, p. 65) (on Asclepius) εὐεργετεῖν ... τοὺς ἀνθρώπους. 38, 15 (7, p. 75) healings are called here τὰς εὐεργεσίας (cf. Acts IV 9). 39, 4 (18, p. 409) (again on Asclepius' healings) ταῖς εὐεργεσίαις ταῖς παρ' αὐτοῦ πεποίηκεν ἁπάντων ἐκφανέστατον (sc. χωρίον). Cf. 50, 68 (26, p. 522) εὐεργεσίας τοῦ θεοῦ. In 37, 19 (2, p. 22) the gods are called εὐεργέται.

Acts X 43 (τούτῳ πάντες οἱ προφῆται μαρτυροῦσιν): Ael. Arist. 46, 7 (3, p. 31) σὺν μάρτυσι τοῖς ποιηταῖς.

Acts XII 11 (ἐν ἑαυτῷ γενόμενος): Ael. Arist. 43, 2 (1, p. 1) οὐκ ἐν ἐμαυτῷ ἦν.

Acts XII 23 (Herod's death as divine punishment): Ael. Arist. 1, 114 (13, p. 206) Darius ἐκ θεοῦ πληγεὶς ... τελευτᾷ, sc. after his attack on Athens in 490 B.C. (for πληγαί of God see the Apoc. passim, e.g. XVI 9).

Acts XIII-XX (the following passages from Ael. Arist. demonstrate the feeling of safety and the ease with which one could travel in the Roman empire): Ael. Arist. 26, 100 (14, p. 365) νῦν γοῦν ἔξεστι καὶ Ἕλληνι καὶ βαρβάρῳ καὶ τὰ αὑτοῦ κομίζοντι καὶ χωρὶς τῶν αὑτοῦ βαδίζειν ὅποι βούλεται ῥᾳδίως, ἀτεχνῶς ὡς ἐκ πατρίδος εἰς πατρίδα ἰόντι κτλ. Cf. also the next paragraph in Arist. (101). 36, 91 (48, p. 474) one can sail everywhere δοθείσης ἀδείας πλεῖν ὑπὸ τῆς νῦν ἡγεμονίας. 35, 37 (9, p. 111-2) οὐ πᾶσα μὲν ἄδεια πᾶσιν <βαδίζειν> ὅποι βούλεταί τις, πάντες δὲ πανταχοῦ λιμένες ἐνεργοί; οὐ τὰ μὲν ὄρη τὴν αὐτὴν ἔχει τοῖς ὁδεύουσιν ἥνπερ αἱ πόλεις τοῖς οἰκοῦσιν αὐτὰς ἀσφάλειαν, χάρις δὲ πάντα ἐπέχει πεδία, πᾶς δὲ διὰ πάντων λέλυται φόβος; ποῖοι μὲν γὰρ πόροι ποταμῶν κεκώλυνται διελθεῖν, τίνες δὲ θαλάττης ἀποκέκλεινται πορθμοί.

Acts XIII 10 (οὐ παύσῃ διαστρέφων τὰς ὁδοὺς τοῦ κυρίου τὰς εὐθείας): Ael. Arist. 29, 31 (40, p. 760) οὐ παύσεσθε στηλιτεύοντες ὑμᾶς αὐτούς.

Acts XIII 25 (ἐπλήρου Ἰωάννης τὸν δρόμον, cf. XX 24 and 2 Tim. IV 7. According to E. Preuschen, *Die Apostelgeschichte*, Tübingen 1912, p. 84, this expression is a Semitism, but the following text from Ael. Arist. shows that this assumption is unnecessary): Ael. Arist. 1, 113 (13, p. 205) ... πῶς οὐ διὰ παντὸς ἂν εἴποι τις ἀφῖχθαι καὶ καθάπερ τοὺς δρομέας τὸ γιγνόμενον πεπληρωκέναι; (*scholia ad loc.* τουτέστι τὸ ὀφειλόμενον τέλος πεπληρωκέναι, δηλονότι τέλος τοῦ δρόμου. ὡς ἐπὶ ἀγῶνος δὲ εἶπε τὴν λέξιν).

Acts XIII 43 (τῇ χάριτι τοῦ θεοῦ, et passim): Ael. Arist. 39, 3 (18, p. 409) τῇ χάριτι τοῦ θεοῦ.

Acts XIV 12: Ael. Arist. 2, 19 (45, p. 5) καλῶ ... Ἑρμῆν λόγιον. 2, 396 (45, p. 135) Zeus Ἑρμῆν κελεύει ῥητορικὴν ἔχοντα ἐλθεῖν εἰς ἀνθρώπους. 37, 21 (2, p. 22) Ἑρμῆν καλεῖ λόγιον καὶ ἀγοραῖον καὶ ἐμπολαῖον. 3, 663 (46, p. 398) ... Δημοσθένους, ὃν ἐγὼ φαίην ἂν Ἑρμοῦ τινος λογίου τύπον εἰς ἀνθρώπους κατελθεῖν.

Acts XIV 15 (... θεὸν ζῶντα ὃς ἐποίησεν τὸν οὐρανὸν καὶ τὴν γῆν καὶ τὴν θάλασσαν καὶ πάντα τὰ ἐν αὐτοῖς, cf. Hebr. I 10, Apoc. XIV 7): Ael. Arist. 43, 7 (1, p. 2) Διός ἐστιν ἔργα ὅσα ἐστὶ πάντα, ... γῆ καὶ θάλαττα καὶ οὐρανός ... See also *ad* XVII 24a.

Acts XIV 17: Ael. Arist. 43, 24 (1, p. 9) ἥ τε οὐρανοῦ καὶ ὄμβρου συνουσία Διός. 43, 25 (1, p. 10) τοῦ μεγάλου ... πάντων εὐεργέτου (sc. Zeus). 43, 26 (1, p. 10) ἁπάντων θεῶν εὐεργεσίαι Διός εἰσιν ἔργον. 43, 30 (1, p. 11) Zeus is called Ὑέτιος. 41, 10 (4, p. 50) Dionysus is καρπῶν ἔφορος καὶ τροφῆς ἀνθρώποις.

Acts XIV 22 (ἐπιστηρίζοντες τὰς ψυχάς): Ael. Arist. 51, 36 (27, p. 543) τὴν ψυχὴν ἐπερρώνυ.

Acts XIV 22 (ἐμμένειν τῇ πίστει, cf. Gal. III 10, Hebr. VIII 9, and also the μένειν ἐν + dative formulas in John, esp. ch. XV): Ael. Arist. 5, 6 (29, p. 554) ... δεῖν τοῖς ἐγνωσμένοις ἐμμένειν. 7, 1 (31, p. 591) τοῖς ὑμετέροις αὐτῶν ἤθεσι καὶ τρόποις ἐμμεῖναι. 8, 13 (32, p. 605) ... ἐμμένοντας τοῖς κειμένοις. 12, 34 (34, p. 655) ἐμμένουσι ταῖς ὑπαρχούσαις πίστεσιν.

Acts XV 23 ('Α. τοῖς/τῷ Β. χαίρειν, XXIII 26, James I 1; this epistolary greeting is found only here in the N.T.): Ael. Arist. 19, 1 (41, p. 762) Αὐτοκράτορι Καίσαρι Μάρκῳ Αὐρηλίῳ ... Αἴλιος Ἀριστ-είδης χαίρειν. 47, 41 (23, p. 455) Ἀριστείδῃ τῷ ἱερεῖ χαίρειν.

Acts XV 28 (ἔδοξεν γὰρ τῷ πνεύματι τῷ ἁγίῳ καὶ ἡμῖν...): Ael. Arist. 3, 311 (46, p. 279) ὅπου γὰρ ταὐτὰ ἔδοξεν ἐκείνῳ (sc. Themistocles) καὶ τῷ θεῷ περὶ σωτηρίας τῶν ὅλων, τί χρὴ λέγειν ἄλλο; 1, 117 (13, p. 207) οὕτω γὰρ θεοῖς τε καὶ Ξέρξῃ δοκεῖν. Cf. 1, 231 (13, p. 260) ἐδόκει τῷ δαίμονι, and 2, 39 (45, p. 12) ἡ δὲ ἀπεκρίνατο ὡς ἐδόκει τῷ θεῷ.

Acts XVI 6b: Ael. Arist. 47, 69 (23, p. 462) ἀπῄειμεν διὰ Μυσίας εἰς Πέργαμον, ἐπισχόντος δὲ ὀνείρατος καθ' ὁδὸν ἔμεινα ἡμέρας πλείους, συνεχῶς τῆς αὐτῆς ὄψεως γιγνομένης.

Acts XVI 16: Ael. Arist. 2, 47 (45, p. 14) ἀεὶ καὶ περὶ παντὸς τὰς Μούσας ἐνοχλοῦσιν (sc. οἱ ποιηταί) δεόμενοι φράσαι σφίσιν, ὡς αὐτοὶ μὲν προφητῶν σχῆμα καὶ τάξιν ἔχοντες, ἐκείνας δὲ μάντεις ἀληθεῖς οὔσας περὶ ἁπάντων.

Acts XVI 25 (προσευχόμενοι ὕμνουν τὸν θεόν): Ael. Arist. 26, 32 (14, p. 336) ὑμνεῖ καὶ σέβει καὶ συνεύχεται διπλῆν εὐχήν. Cf. 40, 1 (5, p. 53).

Acts XVI 34 (πιστεύειν τῷ θεῷ, XXVII 25, Rom. IV 3 = Gal. III 6 = James II 23 (= Gen. XV 6), Tit. III 8, 1 John V 10): Ael. Arist. 10, 38 (39, p. 747) τοῖς θεοῖς τοῖς κοινοῖς τῶν Ἑλλήνων πιστεύσαντες...

Acts XVI 37f. (XXII 25ff.): Ael. Arist. 26, 63 (14, p. 347) τὸ Ῥωμαῖον εἶναι ἐποιήσατε οὐ πόλεως, ἀλλὰ γένους ὄνομα κοινοῦ τινος, καὶ τούτου οὐχ ἑνὸς τῶν πάντων, ἀλλ' ἀντιρρόπου πᾶσι τοῖς λοιποῖς.

Acts XVII 16 (κατείδωλον οὖσαν τὴν πόλιν, sc. Athens; cf. v. 23): Ael. Arist. 1, 354 (13, p. 306) on Athens: νεῴ τε γὰρ ἐνταῦθα οἱ αὐτοὶ μέγιστοι καὶ κάλλιστοι τῶν πανταχοῦ, καὶ ἀγάλματα, ἄνευ τῶν οὐρανίων, τῆς πρώτης τέχνης τὰ πρῶτα, καὶ παλαιὰ καὶ καινά. Cf. ibid. 364 (p. 309) ἁπάντων ... τῶν ἀρίστων αὕτη πατρὶς καὶ σοφίας πάσης καὶ τέχνης ἡγεμών, ὥστε οὐ μόνον τοῖς ἀγάλμασιν, ἀλλὰ καὶ τοῖς ἀγαλματοποιοῖς αὐτοῖς περίεστιν.

Acts XVII 19 (the Areopagus): Ael. Arist. 1, 46 (13, p. 171) nothing can be found beyond the Areopagus, ἀλλ' ὥσπερ τὰ ὕδατα ὅσα μαντικὰ καὶ πνεύματα αὐτόθεν ἰσχυροῖ, οὕτως καὶ οὗτος ὁ χῶρος ὥσπερ ἀνιέναι δοκεῖ τὴν τοῦ δικαίου γνῶσιν ἐναργῆ καὶ τῆς παρὰ τοῖς θεοῖς ὡς δυνατὸν ἐγγυτάτω. Ibid. 47 (p. 172) the Areopagus is a παράδειγμα δικαιοσύνης. The whole of parr. 46-48 (pp. 170-172) deals with the Areopagus and is worth reading. The passages to be quoted now seem to imply that in the Imperial period the Areopagus still functioned as a court (on this old problem see the literature mentioned by W. Bauer in his *Wörterbuch* 208). 1, 367 (13, p. 309f.) εἰ τοίνυν τις ἐρωτῴη ποῖον τῶν ἐν τοῖς Ἕλλησι δικαστηρίων ἐντιμότατον καὶ ἁγιώτατον, τὸ ἐν Ἀρείῳ πάγῳ πάντες ἂν φήσαιεν. ibid. 385 (p. 314) καὶ μὴν εἰς τὴν ἐξ Ἀρείου πάγου βουλὴν βλέψαντα πάντα ἂν ἡγοῦμαι φῆσαι μὴ εἶναι καλλίω λαβεῖν ἀριστοκρατίας εἰκόνα μηδ' ἥτις σῴζει μᾶλλον τοὔνομα (*scholia ad loc.* οἱ ἐν Ἀρείῳ πάγῳ δικάζοντες ἄριστοι καὶ θαυμαστότατοι τῶν ἄλλων πολιτῶν ἦσαν σοφίᾳ τε καὶ φρονήσει καὶ γνώμης ὀρθότητι καὶ ἐπιεικείᾳ).

Acts XVII 21 (ἢ λέγειν τι ἢ ἀκούειν τι): Ael. Arist. 29, 8 (40, p. 753) μηδὲν ἀπηχὲς μήτε λέγειν μήτε ἀκούειν. ibid. 10 (p. 754) τὰ αἴσχιστα ἀκούειν καὶ λέγειν.

Acts XVII 22b: Ael. Arist. 40, 11 (5, p. 58) the city of Athens τῆς εἰς τοὺς θεοὺς εὐσεβείας ... ὥσπερ ἡγεμὼν τοῖς ἅπασιν ὑπῆρχεν.

Acts XVII 24a: Ael. Arist. 43, 7 (1, p. 2) Ζεὺς τὰ πάντα ἐποίησε. 43, 23 (1, p. 9) ἔστιν οὖν πάντων δὴ τῶν ὄντων Ζεὺς αἴτιός τε καὶ δημιουργός, καὶ διὰ τοῦτον ἅπαντα γίγνεται ὅσα τε οὐράνια καὶ ὅσα ἐπίγεια. See also *ad* XIV 15.

Acts XVII 24b (οὐκ ἐν χειροποιήτοις ναοῖς κατοικεῖ): Ael. Arist. 46, 20 (3, p. 36) πᾶσαι μὲν ἀκταί, πάντες δε λιμένες καὶ πάντα μέρη τῆς γῆς καὶ τῆς θαλάττης ἱερὰ Ποσειδῶνος καὶ ἀναθήματα καὶ ἀγάλματα καὶ τεμένη καὶ νεώ. Cf., by way of contrast, 48, 11 (24, p. 468) ἀπῄειμεν οὖν τὴν ἐπὶ Σμύρνης, καὶ μάλα ἐν ἀηδίᾳ ποιούμενοι καὶ νομίζοντες ἄνευ προστάτου γίγνεσθαι καὶ ὡς ἀληθῶς ἐφ' ἡμῶν αὐτῶν πλεῖν, ἐπειδὴ τοῦ ἱεροῦ ἐγιγνόμεθα ἔξω.

Acts XVII 25 (οὐδὲ ... προσδεόμενός τινος): Ael. Arist. 43, 9 (1, p. 3) Zeus οὐδὲν προσεδεήθη ἑτέρου εἰς τὸ εἶναι. 45, 20 (8, p. 90) αὐτάρκη θεόν, sc. Sarapis.

Acts XVII 26a: Ael. Arist. 43, 14 (1, p. 5) ἀνθρώποις δ' ἐπὶ γῆς (sc. Ζεὺς οἰκήσεις ἀπέδωκε).

Acts XVII 26b: Ael. Arist. 26, 26 (14, p. 333) χρόνων τακταῖς περιόδοις. 36, 38 (48, p. 452) ... εἶναι δὲ ὅρους τακτοὺς τῷ θεῷ πρὸς ἄρκτου καὶ μεσημβρίας. 43, 24 (1, p. 9) τοὺς ἑαυτοῦ φυλάττων ὅρους.

Acts XVII 27a: Ael. Arist. 50, 23 (26, p. 508) Εὐάρεστος Κρής, τῶν ἐν φιλοσοφίᾳ διατριβόντων ἐλθὼν ἀπὸ Αἰγύπτου καθ' ἱστορίαν τῶν περὶ τὸν θεόν.

Acts XVII 27b: Ael. Arist. 43, 26 (1, p. 10) πάντα δὲ πανταχοῦ Διὸς μεστὰ καὶ πᾶσιν ἐφ' ἑκάστης πράξεως παρίδρυται.

Acts XVII 28a (ἐν αὐτῷ γὰρ ζῶμεν): Ael. Arist. 43, 23 (1, p. 9) (Ζεὺς ... ζωῆς ... ἐστὶν αἴτιος). In the background here is the supposed etymological connection between Δία and διά (cf. αἴτιος), and between Ζήν and ζῆν (cf. ζωή); on this see O. Weinreich, "ζῆν and διά in der Etymologie des Ζεύς", *Religionsgeschichtliche Studien*, Darmstadt 1968, 409-412.

Acts XVII 28a (ζῶμεν καὶ κινούμεθα): [Ael. Arist.], Ars Rhet. I 2 (Schmid) τὰ ἔμψυχα καὶ κινούμενα.

Acts XVII 28b (τοῦ γὰρ καὶ γένος ἐσμέν): Ael. Arist. 43, 16 (1, p. 6) man is ἐκ τοῦ αὐτοῦ γένους as the gods. 43, 20 (1, p. 8) man has τοῦ γένους τὴν οἰκειότητα with Zeus. 45, 17 (8, p. 89) speaks of man's τὴν πρὸς θεοὺς συγγένειαν.

Acts XVII 30 (... τοῖς ἀνθρώποις πάντας πανταχοῦ ...): Ael. Arist. 1, 45 (3, p. 170) πανταχόθεν πάντας ἀνθρώπους ἐπιστρέφοντες πρὸς τὴν πόλιν. For πάντας πανταχοῦ cf. in the N.T. Acts XXI 28, XXIV 3, 1 Cor. IV 17, IX 22, 2 Cor. IX 8 (!), Eph. V 20, Phil. I 4; and in Ael. Arist. 26, 89 (14, p. 360) δίκης δὲ καὶ αἰδοῦς πάντα πανταχοῦ μεστά. 2, 192 (45, p. 58) πανταχοῦ πάντ' ἐστὶ κτλ. 43, 18 (1, p. 7) πανταχοῦ πᾶσι. 45, 25 (8, p. 93) πανταχῇ πάντας περιέχων. Cf. 2, 297 (45, p. 95) ὅπως ... πάντας πάντ' ἀδικῶν ἐν ἅπασι τοῖς χρόνοις ἐν ἅπασι τοῖς κακοῖς ᾖ.

Acts XVII 31 (πίστιν παρασχών = giving proof): Ael. Arist. 3, 39 (46, p. 119) τῷ δὲ τὸν ἐν τάξει βίον ἀντὶ τοῦ πρὸς ἡδονὴν προῃρῆσθαι σωφροσύνης πίστιν παρείχετο ἐμφανῆ. 7, 11 (31, p. 594) ... πίστιν παρειχόμεθα ... Cf. 43, 2 (1, p. 1) σωφροσύνης ... ἔχει πίστιν.

Acts XIX 20 (κράτος of God, passim): Ael. Arist. 37, 8 (2, p. 15) τὸ μὲν δὴ κράτος τῆς θεοῦ τοσοῦτον ... 45, 32 (8, p. 96) μηδέποτε ἐκφεύγειν ἡμᾶς τὸ τούτου κράτος (sc. of Sarapis).

Acts XIX 23ff.: Ael. Arist. 43, 25 (1, p. 9) Ἥρα ... καὶ Ἄρτεμις ... εὐεργετοῦσιν ἀνθρώπους.

Acts XIX 27: Ael. Arist. 23, 25 (42, p. 776) (πῶς εἰκὸς) ... κατὰ μὲν τοὺς χρόνους τοὺς Περσικοὺς τοσαύτην αἰδῶ παρὰ τῶν βαρβάρων ὑπάρχειν τῇ Ἀτρέμιδι, ἡνίκα δ' αὐτός τε ὁ νεὼς μείζων ἢ πρόσθεν ἕστηκεν, ἀρχή τε ἡ μεγίστη πασῶν καὶ ἅμα σεμνοτάτη καθέστηκεν, μὴ καὶ ἓν τοῦτο ἐξαρκεῖν ὑπολαμβάνειν εἰς φιλίαν τῇ πόλει τὴν τῆς θεοῦ τιμήν, ἣν αὐτή τε τιμήσασα ἔχει τὴν πόλιν (sc. Ephesus) καὶ παρ' ἀνθρώπων αὐτὴν εἰκός ἐστι φέρεσθαι.

Acts XIX 28-34 (... ἔκραζον ... ἡ πόλις ... τὸ θέατρον ... τὸ θέατρον ... ἔκραζον ... ἡ ἐκκλησία ... κραζόντων): Ael. Arist. 30, 9 (10, p. 117) ἡ πόλις αὐτὴ συνομολογεῖ καὶ κέκραγεν ἐν τοῖς βουλευτηρίοις, ἐν τοῖς θεάτροις, ἐν ταῖς ἐκκλησίαις.

Acts XIX 28.34 (μεγάλη ἡ Ἄρτεμις, cf. Tit. II 13): Ael. Arist. 48, 7 (24, p. 467) ἐβόων ... · μέγας ὁ Ἀσκληπιός. ibid. 21 (p. 471) exactly the same expression. Cf. 45, 23 (8, p. 92) μέγας οὗτος ὁ θεός (sc. Sarapis).

Acts XIX 31 (Ἀσιάρχης): Ael. Arist. 50, 53 (26, p. 518): in a dream, Aristides received the title "Asiarch"; on this term see the lit. in Bauer's *Wörterbuch s.v.* and Nilsson, *Gesch. der griech. Rel.* II 386.

Acts XIX 35 (τοῦ διοπετοῦς): Ael. Arist. 1, 354 (13, p. 306) ἀγάλματα, ἄνευ τῶν οὐρανίων (= apart from those which fell from heaven), . . . τὰ πρῶτα.

Acts XX 24 (διακονία in a religious sense, passim): Ael. Arist. 49, 40 (25, p. 499) διακονίᾳ δ' ἡμῶν, i.e. by our sacrifice.

Acts XX 28 (ἐπίσκοποι, Phil. I 1, 1 Tim. III 2, Tit. I 7, 1 Ptr. II 25): Ael. Arist. 23, 79 (42, p. 795) τῶν κατ' ἐνιαυτὸν ἐπισκόπων ἀφικνουμένων, sc. the provincial governors.

Acts XXI 37b: Ael. Arist. 1, 324 (13, p. 294) ταύτην μίαν φωνὴν (sc. the Attic dialect) κοινὴν ἅπαντες τοῦ γένους ἐνόμισαν, καὶ δι' ὑμῶν ὁμόφωνος μὲν πᾶσα γέγονεν ἡ οἰκουμένη, ἴδοις δ' ἂν καὶ τοὺς Ἡνιόχους (a fierce tribe of barbarians living near the Black Sea) καὶ τοὺς νομέας καὶ τοὺς ἀπὸ τῆς θαλάττης ζῶντας καὶ πάντα ὅσα ἔθνη καὶ κατὰ πόλεις καὶ κατὰ χώρας τῆς παρ' ὑμῶν φωνῆς ἐχομένους. ibid. 326 (p. 295) πάντες . . . ἐπὶ τήνδε (sc. φωνήν) ἐληλύθασιν ὥσπερ ὅρον παιδείας νομίζοντες. These texts clearly testify the great expansion of Koine Greek.

Acts XXII 3 (γεγεννημένος . . . ἀνατεθραμμένος . . . πεπαιδευμένος): Ael. Arist. 38, 8 (7, p. 73) οὕτω δὴ φύντες καὶ τραφέντες καὶ παιδευθέντες. 38, 7 (7, p. 73) γενομένους δ' αὐτοὺς τρέφει ὁ πατὴρ . . . καὶ ἐπειδὴ ἐδέχετο ἡ ἡλικία, . . . ἐδίδαξεν αὐτός. 32, 2 (12, p. 134) καὶ τραφεὶς ὑπ' ἐκείνῳ καὶ παιδευθείς . . . 24, 42 (44, p. 837) παίδων τροφαὶ καὶ παιδεία. 1, 368 (13, p. 310) . . . τοὺς δὲ παῖδας δημοσίᾳ τρέφειν ἄχρι ἥβης . . . 30, 4 (10, p. 115) . . . ἐπὶ τῆς αὐτῆς (sc. πόλεως) γνησίως τετράφθαι. 43, 8 (1, p. 2) Κρήτης ἐν εὐώδεσιν ἄντροις τραφείς. See W. C. van Unnik, "Tarsus or Jerusalem, the City of Paul's Youth", *Sparsa Collecta* I, Leiden 1973, 259-320, esp. 274ff.

Acts XXII 25-29: Ael. Arist. 26, 60ff. (14, pp. 346ff.) on Rome's readiness to grant Roman citizenship to whoever merits it. Cf. ibid. 78 (p. 354) ἀλλ' ἐν τιμῆς αὐτοὺς μέρει λήψεσθαι τὴν μετουσίαν τῆς πολιτείας. ibid. 100 (p. 365) εἰς ἀσφάλειαν ἐξαρκεῖ Ῥωμαῖον εἶναι, μᾶλλον δὲ ἕνα τῶν ὑφ' ὑμῖν.

Acts XXIII 11 (τῇ δὲ ἐπιούσῃ νυκτί; in the N.T. only Luke uses ἡ ἐπιοῦσα, others use ἐπαύριον): Ael. Arist. 48, 75 (24, p. 485) τῇ δ' ἐπιούσῃ νυκτὶ ...

Acts XXIII 11 (ἐπιστὰς αὐτῷ ὁ κύριος εἶπεν· Θάρσει): Ael. Arist. 47, 18 (23, p. 449) ἐδόκει μοι παραθαρρύνειν Φοῖβος παρών (also in a dream or a vision).

Acts XXIV 2 (the πρόνοια of the governor): Ael. Arist. 23, 79 (42, p. 795) on the πρόνοια of the governors: ἡμῖν δ' ὅσῳ καὶ διαφερόντως τῶν ἄλλων ὑπάρχει τιμᾶσθαι καὶ ὑπὸ τῶν βασιλέων καὶ ὑπὸ τῶν κατ' ἐνιαυτὸν ἐπισκόπων ἀφικνουμένων, ..., πῶς οὐ καὶ τὴν πρόνοιαν εἰκὸς εἶναι πλείω τοῦ μή τι φαίνεσθαι ποιοῦντας ὃ τούτοις ἂν δόξειεν οὐ καλῶς ἔχειν; μηδαμῶς. 26, 36 (14, p. 337) ἐπὶ προστασίᾳ καὶ προνοίᾳ τῶν ἀρχομένων (also said of governors). 26, 96 (14, p. 364) the Romans are κατὰ πολλὴν φειδώ τε καὶ πρόνοιαν ἐξηγούμενοι. 47, 49 (23, p. 457) (said to the Emperors) χάριν ὑμῖν, ἔφην, ἔχω, αὐτοκράτορες, πάσης προνοίας.

Acts XXIV 14 (τῷ πατρῴω θεῷ): Ael. Arist. 30, 1 (10, p. 113) ... θεοῖς ... πατρῴοις.

Acts XXV 10 (βῆμα Καίσαρος): Ael. Arist. 47, 23 (23, p. 451) καθέζεσθαι δ' αὐτὸν ἐπί τινος βήματος (said of the Emperor).

Acts XXV 11ff.: Ael. Arist. 26, 37-39 (14, pp. 337-8) is a description of the possibility to appeal to the Emperor. Cf. also 50, 96 (26, p. 530) παρ' ἡμῶν ἔφεσις μὲν εἰς Ῥώμην ἐδίδοτο (ἔφεσις = appeal).

Acts XXVI 14 (πρὸς κέντρα λακτίζειν): Ael. Arist. 2, 230 (45, p. 70) καίτοι τό γε πρὸς νόμον καὶ ταῦτα ἀνθρώπων ἅμα καὶ θεῶν βασιλέα μάχεσθαι οὐκ ἦν ἐπαινεῖν πρὸς Πινδάρου (cf. *Pyth.* II 96), οὐδὲ συμβουλεύειν πρὸς κέντρα λακτίζειν.

Acts XXVI 16 (ὑπηρέτης, sc. θεοῦ, 1 Cor. IV 1): Ael. Arist. 43, 22 (1, p. 9) ἀνθρώπους δὲ θεῶν θεραπευτάς τε καὶ ὑπηρέτας.

Acts XXVII 22 (ἐπικουρίας οὖν τυχὼν τῆς ἀπὸ τοῦ θεοῦ): Ael. Arist. 37, 12 (2, p. 17) τῷ γένει τῶν ἀνθρώπων ἐπίκουρος γεγένηται, sc. Athena. 38, 14 (7, p. 75) ἡ παρ' αὐτῶν (sc. the Asclepiads) ἐπικουρία. For τυγχάνειν in the sense of "receiving from God" (also in 2 Tim. II 10, Hebr. XI 35) cf. 1, 33-4, (13, p. 166) δεηθέντας δέ που καὶ τυχεῖν. ... κατ' ἀξίαν τυχεῖν.

Acts XXVII 6: Ael. Arist. 36, 116 (48, p. 485) ... αἱ ὁλκάδες αἱ εἰς Ἰταλίαν ἀπ' Αἰγύπτου πλέουσαι, ἐπειδὰν ἀναπλεύσωσιν ἐκεῖθεν, σῶν ἔχουσι τὸ λοιπὸν οὗ παρεσκευάσαντο.

Acts XXVII 9ff.: Ael. Arist. 48, 65-68 (24, pp. 482-3) is a long description of a storm at sea, which has some parallels in the story of Acts; see W. L. Knox, *Some Hellenistic Elements in Primitive Christianity*, p. 13 n. 3. Some details: compare 67 ἄκοντος ἐμοῦ καὶ ἀντιλέγοντος ἐξ ἀρχῆς and 68 κυβερνήτου καὶ ναυτῶν ... πλεῖν ἀξιούντων καὶ μηδὲν ἀκούειν ἐθελόντων ἐμοῦ with Acts XXVII 10f. 68 ἐναντία τοῖς πλεύμασι with Acts XXVII 4. 68 τέτταρες πάλιν αὗται πρὸς ταῖς δέκα ἡμέραι καὶ νύκτες χειμῶνος, κύκλῳ διὰ παντὸς τοῦ πελάγους φερομένων with Acts XXVII 27 and 33. 68 ἀσιτίαι οὐκ ὀλίγαι with Acts XXVII 21 and 33. Cf. also 50, 33 (26, p. 511) ὡς γὰρ ἐξέβην εἰς τὴν Δῆλον, ἀχθεσθεὶς τῷ κυβερνήτῃ, ταραχώδει τε ὄντι καὶ ὑπεναντία τοῖς ἀνέμοις πλέοντι καὶ οἷον ἀροῦντι τὸ πέλαγος, εὐθὺς ὅρκῳ καταλάμβανω, ἦ μὴν μήτε ἐκπλεύσεσθαι δυοῖν ἡμερῶν, ἀλλ' εἰ φίλον αὐτῷ, πλείτω, ἔφην, ἐφ' ἑαυτοῦ. See also the texts quoted *ad* Acts XXVII 13-44.

Acts XXVII 13-44: Ael. Arist. 45, 33 (8, p. 97) (said to Sarapis) ἐπιρρεούσης τῆς θαλάττης καὶ πολλῆς πάντοθεν αἰρομένης καὶ οὐδενὸς ὁρωμένου πλὴν τοῦ μέλλοντος καὶ σχεδὸν ἤδη παρόντος ὀλέθρου χεῖρα ἀντάρας οὐρανόν τε κεκρυμμένον ἐξέφηνας καὶ γῆν ἔδωκας ἰδεῖν καὶ προσορμίσασθαι, τοσοῦτον παρ' ἐλπίδα ὥστ' οὐδ' ἐπιβᾶσι πίστις ἦν. 48, 12 (24, p. 468) καὶ ἐπειδὴ ἦμεν περὶ τὰς νήσους Δρυμοῦσαν καὶ Πήλην, αὔρα τις εὔρου ὑπήρχετο καὶ περαιτέρω προϊόντων εὖρος ἤδη λαμπρὸς καὶ τέλος ἐξερράγη πνεῦμα ἐξαίσιον. καὶ τὸ πλοῖον ἐκ πρῴρας ἀρθὲν ἐπὶ πρύμναν ὤκλασεν καὶ μικροῦ κατέδυ. ἔπειτα ἐπεκλύζετο ἔνθεν καὶ ἔνθεν. ἔπειτα ἀπεστράφη ἔξω πρὸς τὸ πέλαγος. ἱδρὼς δὲ καὶ θόρυβος ναυτῶν καὶ βοαὶ πᾶσαι τῶν ἐμπλεόντων—συνέπλεον γὰρ δὴ καὶ τῶν ἐπιτηδείων τινές—, ἐμοὶ δὲ τοσοῦτον ἤρκεσεν εἰπεῖν· 'ὦ Ἀσκληπιέ'. πολλὰ δὲ καὶ παντοῖα κινδυνεύσαντες καὶ τέλος περὶ αὐτὴν τὴν καταγωγὴν μυριάκις ἀνατραπέντες καὶ ἀπωσθέντες καὶ πολλὴν ἀγωνίαν τοῖς ὁρῶσι παρασχόντες διεσώθημεν ἀγαπητῶς καὶ μόλις. Cf. 43, 25 (1, p. 10) Ποσειδῶν τε καὶ Διόσκουροι σῴζουσι τοὺς πλέοντας.

Acts XXVII 21-26.33f.: Ael. Arist. 49, 43 (25, p. 499) ἰδὼν ἱκετεύοντας καὶ τεταραγμένους τοὺς ἀνθρώπους ἐμέλλησα μὲν εἰπεῖν ὡς οὐδὲν δέοι δεδιέναι, οὐδὲν γὰρ ἔσεσθαι δυσχερές· οὐ γὰρ ἂν αὐτὸς ἐπὶ τούτοις εἰς τὴν πόλιν κληθῆναι.

Acts XXVII 22.25.36 (εὐθυμεῖν, cf. James V 13): Ael. Arist. 48, 23 (24, p. 471) ἦν τις ἄρρητος εὐθυμία, πάντα δεύτερα τοῦ παρόντος καιροῦ τιθεμένη, ὥστε οὐδ' ὁρῶν τὰ ἄλλα ἐδόκουν ὁρᾶν. οὕτω πᾶς ἦν πρὸς τῷ θεῷ.

Acts XXVII 23f.: Ael. Arist. 50, 37 (26, p. 513) ..., τὸν δὲ θεὸν προειδότα ἐφ' ἅπασι τοῖς μέλλουσι σημῆναι τοῦτο μὲν ὡς ἐν θαλάττῃ κίνδυνοί τε συμβήσονται καὶ ἐξ αὐτῶν σωτηρίαι.

Acts XXVIII 11 (πλοίῳ ... 'Αλεξανδρίνῳ παρασήμῳ Διοσκούροις): Ael. Arist. 43, 25 (1, p. 10) Διόσκουροι σῴζουσι τοὺς πλέοντας.

ROMANS

Rom. I 1 (εὐαγγέλιον θεοῦ, etc.): Ael. Arist. 53, 3 (55, p. 708) Ζεὺς Εὐαγγέλιος (Zeus giver of glad tidings).

Rom. I 1 (κλητός, sc. ὑπὸ τοῦ θεοῦ, cf. vv. 6 and 7; esp. 1 Cor. VII 15-24, et al.): Ael. Arist. 30. 9 (10, p. 116) ὁ δ' ὑπὸ τοῦ θεοῦ κληθεὶς ὡς ἀναληψόμενος τὴν πόλιν ὑπὸ χρόνου κεκμηκυῖαν.

Rom. I 8 (πρῶτον μὲν γὰρ ..., not followed by δεύτερον δέ, ἔπειτα δέ or εἶτα δέ, as in III 2 and 1 Cor. XI 18): Ael. Arist. 12, 19 (34, p. 649) πρῶτον μὲν γὰρ ..., not resumed; the same in 2, 33 (45, p. 10).

Rom. I 9 (μάρτυς γάρ μού ἐστιν ὁ θεός, 2 Cor. I 23, Phil. I 8, 1 Thess. II 5.10): Ael. Arist. 16, 31 (52, p. 603) οὐκ αἰσχύνει τοὺς θεοὺς αὐτοὺς μάρτυρας τοσαύτης κακίας ποιούμενος.

Rom. I 14 (Ἕλλησίν τε καὶ βαρβάροις): Ael. Arist. 1, 4 (13, p. 152) πρὸς Ἕλληνας καὶ βαρβάρους. 1, 92 (13, p. 195) τοῖς Ἕλλησι καὶ βαρβάροις. 1, 157 (13, p. 226) Ἕλληνας ὁμοῦ καὶ βαρβάρους. 2, 68 (45, p. 22) οὐ μόνον τῶν Ἑλλήνων ἀλλὰ καὶ βαρβάρων. 3, 287 (46, p. 270) ... τῆς ἀρετῆς τῆς ἐκείνου φανερᾶς ἅπασιν Ἕλλησι καὶ βαρβάροις γεγονυίας. 36, 88 (48, p. 473) ... οὔτε Ἑλλήνων οὔτε βαρβάρων οὐδένες. Further 1, 172 (13, p. 233), 3, 392 (46, p. 310), 26, 41 (14, p. 338), 26, 63 (14, p. 347), 35, 36 (9, p. 111), 38, 12 (7, p. 75), *et al.*

Rom. I 19ff.: Ael. Arist. 45, 15 (8, p. 88) οὐ γὰρ ἀλλοῖός ἐστιν ἢ οἷος ἐκ τῶν ἔργων ἐπιφαίνεται καὶ δείκνυται, sc. Sarapis.

Rom. I 20 (τὰ γὰρ ἀόρατα ... νοούμενα καθορᾶται): Ael. Arist. 43, 7 (1, p. 2) Zeus made every visible thing καὶ ὅσα δεῖ νοήσει λαβεῖν.

Rom. I 23 (ἤλλαξαν τὴν δόξαν κτλ.): Ael. Arist. 1, 313 (13, p. 291) Athens οὐχ ἡδονὰς ἀντὶ τῶν δικαίων ἠλλάξατο.

Rom. I 26 (αἵ ... θήλειαι ... μετήλλαξαν τὴν φυσικὴν χρῆσιν): Ael. Arist. 1, 83 (13, p. 189) the Amazones παρῆλθον τοῖς ἔργοις τὴν φύσιν (*schol. ad loc.* οὐ γὰρ οἰκεῖον ταῖς γυναιξὶν ὅπλα φέρειν καὶ ἀνδρίζεσθαι). See also the reference to ἡ φύσις in 1 Cor. XI 14f. and Ael. Arist. 26, 20 (14, p. 331) quoted *ad* Rom. II 14.

Rom. I 29ff. ("Lasterkatalog", cf. Gal. V 19ff., Eph. IV 31, Col. III 8, etc.): Ael. Arist. 26 20, (14, p. 331) μίση καὶ ἐπιβουλὰς ἐκ τῶν οὕτω διατιθεμένων καὶ ἀποστάσεις καὶ μάχας ἐν ἀλλήλοις καὶ συνεχεῖς ἔριδας καὶ ἀπαύστους φιλονικίας. Cf. 24, 32 (44, p. 834) ... ὀργὴν ... θυμῷ ... φθόνον ... πλεονεξίαν.

Rom. II 1.3 (ὦ ἄνθρωπε ...): Ael. Arist. 11, 26 (33, p. 622) ἄνθρωπε, ἀκολουθῶ τῇ χρείᾳ ... 12, 54 (34, p. 663) ἄνθρωπε, ῥιπτεῖς ἔχων;

Rom. II 6 (ἀποδώσει ἑκάστῳ κατὰ τὰ ἔργα αὐτοῦ, 2 Tim. IV 14, Apoc. XX 12f., etc.): Ael. Arist. 45, 25 (8, p. 93) in the hereafter χώρους τε ὁ διαιρῶν ἑκάστοις οὗτός (sc. Sarapis) ἐστιν πρὸς ἀξίαν τῆς ἐν τῇ γῇ διαίτης.

Rom. II 8 (ὀργὴ καὶ θυμός, Eph. IV 31, Col. III 8; cf. Apoc. XIV 10, XVI 19, XIX 15): [Ael. Arist.] 35, 10 (9, p. 101) μηδὲ ὀξύρροπον εἶναι πρός τε ὀργὴν καὶ θυμόν. 27, 34 (16, p. 396) the emperors M. Antoninus and L. Verus οὐ θυμοῦ ῥώμην οὐδὲ ὀργῆς ἀμετρίαν τὰ ἐπίσημα τῆς ἀρχῆς ἐποιήσαντο.

Rom. II 14 (φύσει ... νόμου): Ael. Arist. 1, 390 (13, p. 316) καὶ γάρ τοι μόνη πόλεων οὐ μετέθηκε τὸν θεσμὸν οὐδ' ἐποίησε τὰ τῇ φύσει τρίτα τῷ νόμῳ πρῶτα. 24, 35 (44, p. 835) νόμος γάρ ἐστιν οὗτος φύσει κείμενος ὡς ἀληθῶς ὑπὸ τῶν κρειττόνων καταδειχθείς, ἀκούειν τὸν ἥττω τοῦ κρείττονος. Cf. 28, 125 (49, p. 531) ... τὸν τῆς φύσεως νόμον. 26, 20 (14, p. 331) ἃ τούτοις αὖ παρέπεσθαι <ὁ> φύσεως νόμος διέταξε.

Rom. II 19f.: Ael. Arist. 1, 330 (13, p. 296-7) Aristides says to the Athenians: ἀτεχνῶς πάντας ἀνθρώπους καὶ πάντα γένη τῇ καλλίστῃ τῶν εὐεργεσιῶν ἀνέχετε, ἡγεμόνες παιδείας καὶ σοφίας ἁπάσης γιγνόμενοι καὶ πάντας ἁπανταχοῦ καθαίροντες. τῇ μὲν γὰρ τῶν Ἐλευσινίων τελετῇ τοῖς εἰσαφικνουμένοις ἐξηγηταὶ τῶν ἱερῶν μυσταγωγοὶ κέκλησθε, διὰ παντὸς δὲ τοῦ χρόνου πᾶσιν ἀνθρώποις τῶν εἰς τὸ μέσον εἰσφορῶν ἱερῶν ἐξηγηταὶ καὶ διδάσκαλοι καθεστήκατε.

Rom. III 4 (μὴ γένοιτο, passim in Paul): Ael. Arist. 1, 335 (13, p. 299) ἀλλὰ μὴν πέντε μέν ἐστι μνήμη βασιλειῶν, μὴ γένοιτο δὲ πλειόνων. 6, 22 (30, p. 578) μηδὲ γὰρ γένοιτο, ὦ Ζεῦ καὶ πάντες θεοί. 7, 13 (31, p. 595) εἰ δ', ὃ μὴ γένοιτο, σφαλείημεν ... Also 10, 35 (39, p. 746) and 23, 80 (42, p. 795).

Rom. III 5 (κατὰ ἄνθρωπον, only in Paul, 1 Cor. III 3, IX 8, XV 32, Gal. I 11, III 15): Ael. Arist. 48, 8 (24, p. 467) τὰ δ' ἐντεῦθεν ἔστι μὲν οὐ κατ' ἄνθρωπον διηγήσασθαι, ἐγχειρητέον δέ. 1, 301 (13, p. 285) κρεῖττον ἢ κατ' ἄνθρωπον. The same expression also in 31, 15 (11, p. 131), 31, 19 (11, p. 133), 27, 16 (16, p. 389), 27, 21 (16, p. 391).

Rom. III 9 (τί οὖν; VI 15, XI 7): Ael. Arist. 28, 17 (49, p. 496) τρεῖς καὶ εἴκοσι, φησί, πόλεις εἷλον;—τί οὖν; οὗτος αὐτὸς τὰς ἁπάσας; This expression occurs also in 9, 12 (38, p. 715), 16, 12 (52, p. 590), 2, 254 (45, p. 79), 2, 293 (45, p. 79). See R. Bultmann, *Der Stil der paulinischen Predigt und die ... Diatribe*, 1910, 14.65.101.

Rom. III 19 (ὁ νόμος λέγει, 1 Cor. IX 8, XIV 34): Ael. Arist. 1, 110 (13, p. 203) τοὺς μὲν γὰρ ἄλλους τὰ τροφεῖα κομίζεσθαι παρὰ τῶν ἐκτραφέντων ὁ νόμος λέγει, i.e. the unwritten law.

Rom. IV 18 (παρ' ἐλπίδα): Ael. Arist. 7, 2 (31, p. 591) παρ' ἀξίαν ἢ παρ' ἐλπίδας εὐτυχοῦσιν.

Rom. V 5 (ἡ ἀγάπη τοῦ θεοῦ, passim): Ael. Arist. 1, 41 (13, p. 169) νικᾷ μὲν Ἀθηνᾶ ..., Ποσειδῶν δὲ ὑπεχώρησε μέν, οὐ μὴν κατέλυσε τὸν ἔρωτα (Poseidon's love for the Athenians is called ἔρως, whereas God's love in the N.T. is called ἀγάπη).

Rom. V 6.7.8 (ἀποθανεῖν ὑπέρ τινος): Ael. Arist. 51, 25 (27, p. 540) ἀπέθανεν ... ἀντ' ἐμοῦ. See further *ad* Mk. X 45b.

Rom. VI 5 (σύμφυτος): Ael. Arist. 11, 34 (33, p. 625) σύμφυτόν ἐστι τῇ πόλει ταύτῃ πάλαι τὸ παρὰ πᾶσιν εὐδοκιμοῦν.

Rom. VI 8 (συζήσομεν αὐτῷ, sc. Χριστῷ, cf. 2 Cor. VII 3, 2 Tim. II 11): Ael. Arist. 46, 9 (3, p. 32) παρέχων ἑαυτῷ (sc. Ποσειδῶνι) συζῆν καὶ συνεῖναι καὶ συμπολιτεύεσθαι.

Rom. VII 8 (ἀφορμή metaphorically used, VII 11, 2 Cor. V 12, XI 12, Gal. V 13, 1 Tim. V 14): Ael. Arist. 1, 107 (13, p. 202) νομίσαντες ὥσπερ ἀφορμὴν εἰληφέναι παρὰ τῆς τύχης κτλ. 5, 38 (29, p. 566) ... καὶ κατέχει ῥᾳδίως ἀφορμῇ τῷ φόβῳ χρώμενος. 25, 12 (43, p. 801) ἐστὲ δὲ οὐκ ἀτυχημάτων ἐνδεεῖς, ὥστε προστιθέναι τούτοις, ἀλλ' ἀφαιροῦντες μᾶλλον τῶν συμβεβηκότων καὶ τῆς ἐγχωρούσης ἀεὶ ποριζόμενοι ῥᾳστώνης ἀφορμὰς εὖ φρονοῖτ' ἂν καὶ ποιοῖτε ἃ δεῖ. 26, 85 (14, p. 358) ... τὰς δὲ πράξεις ἀφορμὰς ὧν εὔχονται νομίζειν.

Rom. VIII 6 (τὸ φρόνημα τῆς σαρκός, τὸ φρόνημα τοῦ πνεύματος): Ael. Arist. 12, 8 (34, p. 645) ... καὶ τὸ τῆς πόλεως φρόνημα σῴζοντες, οὕτως ἤδη πάντας ὅσους οἷοί τε ἦσαν παραλαβόντες πόλεμον ἐξήνεγκαν.

Rom. VIII 8 (θεῷ ἀρέσκειν, 1 Thess. II 15, IV 1; cf. ἀρεστός, εὐάρεστος, εὐαρεστέω): Ael. Arist. 3, 609 (46, p. 380) πολιτικὰ καὶ ἀνθρώπινα καὶ θεοῖς ἀρέσκοντα.

Rom. VIII 15 (πνεῦμα δουλείας ... εἰς φόβον): [Ael. Arist.] 35, 21 (9, p. 105) ἅπαν τὸ ὑπήκοον καὶ ὑπὸ φόβου δεδουλωμένον.

Rom. VIII 17 (συμπάσχομεν): Ael. Arist. 40, 22 (5, p. 62) παρεκελεύετο (sc. ὁ θεός) δὲ ἀνέχεσθαι τὰ συμπίπτοντα, ἐπειδή γε καὶ Ἡρακλῆς Διὸς παῖς ὢν ἠνέσχετο.

Rom. VIII 22 (πᾶσα ἡ κτίσις ... συνωδίνει): Ael. Arist. 3, 215 (46, p. 241) δέκα μὲν γὰρ ἑξῆς ἔτη ὤδινεν ἅπασα ἡ ἤπειρος, φιλονεικοῦντες ἅπαντες ἄνθρωποι δίκην τῆς Μαραθῶνι μάχης λαβεῖν.

Rom. VIII 23 (ἀπαρχή metaphorically used, passim): Ael. Arist. 50, 15 (26, p. 506) ἀπάρξασθαι ... τῶν αὐτοσχεδίων δὴ τούτων λόγων.

Rom. VIII 30 (οὓς δὲ προώρισεν, τούτους καὶ ἐκάλεσεν· καὶ οὓς ἐκάλεσεν, τούτους καὶ ἐδικαίωσεν· οὓς δὲ ἐδικαίωσεν, τούτους καὶ ἐδόξασεν. A comparable concatenation can be found in 2 Peter I 5-7): Ael. Arist. 3, 172 (46, p. 222) ἂν ἡ πόλις εὐνομῆται, ἀνάγκη τοὺς οἰκοῦντας αὐτὴν πάντας εὐνόμους εἶναι, καὶ ἄνδρας καὶ γυναῖκας. εἰ δ' εὐνόμους, εὐτάκτους· εἰ δ' εὐτάκτους, σώφρονας· εἰ δὲ σώφρονας, καὶ φρονίμους. φρονίμων δ' ὄντων ἁπάντων οὐχ οἷόν τε δήπουθεν ἁμαρτάνειν οὐδένα. 3, 559 (46, p. 364) εἰ δὲ εὐσχημόνως, καὶ τεταγμένως· εἰ δὲ τεταγμένως, καὶ κοσμίως.

Rom. IX 3 (ὑπὲρ τῶν ἀδελφῶν μου, this vicarious ὑπέρ passim): Ael. Arist. 1, 53 (13, p. 176) (on Athens' activities on behalf of the sons of Heracles) ἃ μὲν κατειργάσατο μετ' αὐτῶν καὶ ὑπὲρ αὐτῶν ἐν ἑτέρᾳ τῶν λόγων καθήκει δηλῶσαι μερίδι. ibid. 133 (p. 215) ... Ἀθηναίους ὑπὲρ σφῶν ἀγωνίζεσθαι. Cf. ibid. 138 (p. 218), 141 (p. 220), 197 (p. 244).

Rom. IX 17 (God says: ... ὅπως ἐνδείξωμαι ἐν σοὶ τὴν δύναμίν μου): Ael. Arist. 48, 55 (24, p. 479) τοῦ θεοῦ ... τὴν αὐτοῦ δύναμιν καὶ πρόνοιαν ἐμφανίζοντος.

Rom. IX 19 (ἐρεῖς μοι οὖν· ... The fictive interlocutor or hypothetic opponent, also found in 1 Cor. XV 35 ἀλλὰ ἐρεῖ τις, and James II 18): Ael. Arist. 12, 41 (34, p. 658) ἀλλ' ὦ μάτην δεδιώς, ἡ χάρις αὐτούς, ἣν ὀφείλουσι τῆς βοηθείας ἡμῖν, μετριωτέρους ποιήσει, φαίη τις ἄν. 34, 38 (50, p. 560) νὴ Δί', εἴποι τις ἄν, ἀλλ' ἠκολούθησαν κτλ.

Rom. X 2 (ζῆλον θεοῦ ἔχουσι): Ael. Arist. 1, 338 (13, p. 301) ἡ περὶ τοὺς θεοὺς σπουδή.

Rom. X 7 (ἐκ νεκρῶν ἀναγαγεῖν, Hebr. XIII 20): Ael. Arist. 40, 7 (5, p. 55) τὸν Κέρβερον ὡς ἀνήγαγεν ἐξ Ἅιδου.

Rom. XI 20 (ὑψηλὰ φρονεῖν, XII 16, 1 Tim. VI 17; cf. Rom. XII 3): Ael. Arist. 46, 25 (3, p. 38) τῶν μέγα ἐφ' ἑαυτοῖς φρονούντων.

Rom. XI 25 (τὸ πλήρωμα τῶν ἐθνῶν): Ael. Arist. 1, 233 (13, p. 262) πλήρωμα ἔθνους, sc. the whole of the 20.000 slaves who deserted to Deceleia in the Peloponnesian war. Cf. 26, 76 (14, p. 353).

Rom. XI 33 (ὦ βάθος ... σοφίας): Ael. Arist. 36, 70 (48, p. 466) ὦ σοφίας κεφάλαιον.

Rom. XI 33 (ἀνεξερεύνητα τὰ κρίματα αὐτοῦ, sc. of God): Ael. Arist. 45, 25 (8, p. 93) ἀθεάτους ... κρίσεις ποιούμενος, sc. Sarapis.

Rom. XI 34 (τίς σύμβουλος αὐτοῦ (sc. θεοῦ) ἐγένετο;): Ael. Arist. 37, 5 (2, p. 14) σύμβουλον τὴν Ἀθηνᾶν παρεκαθίσατο, sc. Zeus.

Rom. XI 36 (ἐξ αὐτοῦ ... τὰ πάντα, 1 Cor. VIII 6): Ael. Arist. 43, 9 (1, p. 3) πάντα εἶναι ἀπ' ἐκείνου ἤρξατο ... ἐκ Διὸς πάντα. See further *ad* Hebr. II 10.

Rom. XII 3 (ὑπερφρονεῖν παρ' ὃ δεῖ φρονεῖν): Ael. Arist. 1, 199 (13, p. 245-6) ... τοὺς ὑβριστὰς καὶ μεῖζον τῆς φύσεως φρονοῦντας.

Rom. XII 4f. (σῶμα to denote a community, 1 Cor. X 17, XII 12ff., Eph. IV 25): Ael. Arist. 17, 9 (15, p. 374f.) μίαν δ' οὖν (sc. πόλιν) ὁμόχρουν καὶ σύμφωνον ἑαυτῇ καθάπερ ἀνθρώπου σῶμα συμβαίνοντα τῷ ὅλῳ τὰ μέρη παρεχομένην. 21, 5 (22, p. 441) καὶ τὸ δὴ μέγιστον σύμβολον τῆς πόλεως, τὴν διὰ πάντων ὁμολογίαν μουσικὴν ἕν τι τὸ πᾶν σῶμα ἀποφαίνουσαν. 24, 39 (44, p. 836) τὸ κοινὸν σῶμα τῆς πόλεως.

Rom. XII 13 (τὴν φιλοξενίαν διώκοντες, XVI 23, 1 Tim. III 2, V 10, Tit. I 8, Hebr. XIII 2, 1 Ptr. IV 9): Ael. Arist. 1, 50 (13, p. 173) μεγίστη δὲ καὶ κοινοτάτη τῶν εὐεργεσιῶν ἡ τῶν πανταχόθεν δυστυχούντων ὑποδοχὴ καὶ παραμυθία.

Rom. XII 16 (τὸ αὐτὸ ... φρονοῦντες, XV 5, 2 Cor. XIII 11, Phil. II 2, IV 2, cf. Gal. V 10): Ael. Arist. 2, 197 (45, p. 60) ἀπέχουσι τοῦ ταὐτὰ φρονεῖν ἀλλήλοις. 3, 242 (46, p. 253) ὁ μὲν (sc. Τέρπανδρος) γὰρ ἐφ' ἑαυτῶν τοὺς Λακεδαιμονίους ὁμονοεῖν ἐποίησεν, ὁ δ' (sc. Θεμιστοκλῆς) Ἀθηναίους καὶ Λακεδαιμονίους τότε ταὐτὸν ἔπεισε φρονῆσαι, μᾶλλον δ' ἅπαντας τοὺς Ἕλληνας μιᾶς γενέσθαι γνώμης (for μία γνώμη see *ad* Apoc. XVII 13 and 17). 5, 9 (29, p. 555) ... συμμίκτους εἶναι τοὺς ἔχοντας αὐτὴν (sc. Σικελίαν) καὶ μὴ ταὐτὸν φρονεῖν. 24, 8 (44, p. 827) εἰ μία τῶν καθ' ἕνα ἐστὶν οἰκιῶν σωτηρία τὸ ταὐτὰ φρονεῖν, πολὺ μᾶλλον τὰς πόλεις οὕτω δεῖν ἔχειν. See further 5, 47 (29, p. 569), 6, 26 (30, p. 579), 13, 12 (35, p. 674), 23, 65 (42, p. 790), 24, 6 (44, p. 826), 24, 29 (44, p. 833), 24, 38 (44, p. 836), 24, 49 (44, p. 840), 27, 43 (16, p. 399), 32, 2 (12, p. 134); see esp. the whole of Or. 23 (42) Περὶ ὁμονοίας ταῖς πόλεσιν and 24 (44) Ῥοδίοις περὶ ὁμονοίας. From all these passages it is clear that τὸ αὐτὸ φρονεῖν (just like μία γνώμη) is a political term.

Rom. XII 19-21: Ael. Arist. 23, 71 (42, p. 792) οὐ γὰρ ἅπασα νίκη καλὴ οὐδ' ἐκ θεῶν ἀνθρώποις παραγίγνεται.

Rom. XIII 1b: Ael. Arist. 20, 1 (21, p. 429) οἱ θεῶν γνώμῃ βασιλεῖς.

Rom. XIII 2 (ἡ τοῦ θεοῦ διαταγή, 1 Cor. IX 14 ὁ κύριος διέταξεν): Ael. Arist. 45, 8 (8, p. 85) τὴν τῶν θεῶν διάταξιν καὶ βούλησιν.

Rom. XIII 4 (θεοῦ διάκονος, passim): Ael. Arist. 39, 11 (18, p. 411) διάκονόν τε καὶ συνεργὸν τοῦ φιλανθρωποτάτου τῶν θεῶν.

Rom. XV 6 (ὁμοθυμαδὸν ἐν ἑνὶ στόματι): Ael. Arist. 51, 40 (27, p. 544) ὥσπερ ἐξ ἑνὸς στόματος πάντες παραμένειν τε ἐκέλευον.

Rom. XV 11 (only here ἐπαινεῖν with God as object): Ael. Arist. 40, 1 (5, p. 53) ὦ φίλτατε Ἡράκλεις, σέ γε ἐπαινεῖν ἄθλων ὁ ἥδιστος.

Rom. XV 12 (ἀρχεῖν said of God): Ael. Arist. 41, 8 (4, p. 50) ... ἁπάσης (sc. γῆς) αὐτὸν ἄρχοντα, sc. Dionysus; also said of Zeus in 43, 19 (1, p. 8).

Rom. XV 13 (ὁ δὲ θεὸς ... πληρώσαι ὑμᾶς πάσης χαρᾶς) Ael. Arist. 45, 26 (8, p. 93) Σαράπιδος μνησθεὶς ἀνὴρ εὐθυμίας ἅμα καὶ δέους ἐμπίπλαται.

Rom. XV 20 (θεμέλιον as metaphor, 1 Cor. III 10-12): Ael. Arist. 1, 65 (13, p. 182) ταύτης δὲ τοιαύτης (sc. πόλεως) ὥσπερ κρηπῖδος ἢ ῥίζης ὑποκειμένης ἐξεφοίτησαν καὶ διὰ πάσης ἤδη γῆς αἱ τῶν Ἑλλήνων ἀποικίαι (for ῥίζα cf. Rom. XI 16-18).

Rom. XV 28 (σφραγισάμενος): Ael. Arist. 1, 313 (13, p. 291) ὃ δ' ὥσπερεὶ κεφάλαιον τῶν χρόνων ἐκείνων ἐστὶ καὶ ὃ πάσας τῇ πόλει καὶ τὰς ἄνω καὶ τὰς τότε πράξεις ἐπεσφραγίσατο, κτλ.

Rom. XVI 1f. (2 Cor. III 1, Philemon): Ael. Arist. 50, 71-93 (26, pp. 523-529) is a long passage about letters of recommendation.

1 CORINTHIANS

1 + 2 Cor.: Ael. Arist. 46, 20-31 (3, pp. 36-42) is a panegyric on the city of Corinth.

1 Cor. I 22 (Ἕλληνες σοφίαν ζητοῦσιν): Ael. Arist. 1, 330 (13, p. 296) the Athenians are ἡγεμόνες παιδείας καὶ σοφίας ἁπάσης. 26, 41 (14, p. 338) τὸ τοὺς μὲν βαρβάρους ταῖς περιουσίαις καὶ ταῖς δυνάμεσιν ὑπερβαλέσθαι, τοὺς δὲ Ἕλληνας σοφίᾳ καὶ σωφροσύνῃ παρελθεῖν. Cf. ibid. 51 (p. 342).

1 Cor. I 24 (Χριστὸν θεοῦ δύναμιν): Ael. Arist. 37, 28 (2, p. 27) calls the goddess Athena δύναμιν τοῦ Διός. (Cf. Acts VIII 10, where Simon Magus calls himself ἡ δύναμις τοῦ θεοῦ).

1 Cor. I 26-28 (here Paul uses the stylistic device of *repetitio* by saying three times οὐ πολλοί and three times ἐξελέξατο, and twice ἵνα καταισχύνῃ): Ael. Arist. 44, 16 (17, p. 406) the Aegean sea is μεστὸς μὲν λιμένων, μεστὸς δὲ ἱερῶν, μεστὸς δ' αὐλῶν καὶ παιάνων καὶ πηγῶν καὶ ποταμῶν ...

1 Cor. I 26 (contrast-parallel): Ael. Arist. 26, 59 (14, p. 346) τὸ μὲν χαριέστερόν τε καὶ γενναιότερον καὶ δυνατώτερον πανταχοῦ πολιτικὸν ἢ καὶ ὁμόφυλον πᾶν ἀπεδείξατε. 46, 39 (3, p. 45) Leukothea ἔσῳζεν ... πάντας ὁπόσοις σοφίας ἔρως ἦν.

1 Cor. II 1 (ἦλθον οὐ καθ' ὑπεροχὴν λόγου ἢ σοφίας): Ael. Arist. 1, 397 (13, p. 318): isn't the city of Athens praiseworthy in every respect? ἀλλ' ἐν τῇ τῶν λόγων ἀσκήσει καὶ τῆς λοιπῆς σοφίας; ἀλλ' ἔτι καὶ νῦν ἐνταῦθα πάντες συνέρχονται. 30, 5 (10, p. 115) τῇ περὶ λόγους καὶ σοφίαν σπουδῇ.

1 Cor. III 9 (θεοῦ συνεργοί, Col. IV 11, 1 Thess. III 2): Ael. Arist. 40, 2 (5, p. 53) Ἡρακλῆς συνεργὸς τῷ πατρί.

1 Cor. III 18 (μηδεὶς ἑαυτὸν ἐξαπατάτω, Eph. V 6 μηδεὶς ὑμᾶς ἀπατάτω): Ael. Arist. 2, 93 (45, p. 30) μηδείς σε ... ἐξαπατάτω.

1 Cor. IV 21 (πνεύματί τε πραΰτητος, cf. 1 Ptr. III 4): Ael. Arist. 30, 17 (10, p. 120) τὸ ... τῆς ψυχῆς πρᾶον.

1 Cor. VI 7-8: Ael. Arist. 2, 261 (45, p. 81) ἀλλ' ἀδικεῖσθαι βέλτιον ἢ ἀδικεῖν. ἔστω ταῦτα. ἆρα οὖν ὥσπερ βέλτιον, οὕτω καὶ καθάπαξ αἱρετόν; οὔ. φησὶ (sc. Plato) γοῦν οὐδέτερον βούλεσθαι, δῆλον ὅτι καὶ τὸ ἀδικεῖσθαι κακὸν ἡγούμενος, ὀρθῶς, οἶμαι, καὶ γιγνώσκων καὶ λέγων. See also the then following discussion.

1 Cor. VII 10 (παραγγέλλω with God as subject): Ael. Arist. 50, 16 (26, p. 506) εἴ τι ... εἴη παρηγγελκὼς ὁ θεός.

1 Cor. IX 9 (μὴ τῶν βοῶν μέλει τῷ θεῷ;): Ael. Arist. 51, 34 (27, p. 542) καὶ τούτων ἐμέλησε τῷ θεῷ.

1 Cor. IX 24: Ael. Arist. 1, 402 (13, p. 319) τῶν γὰρ 'Αθηναίων νικώντων παρ' ὑμῖν ἐστι τὸ νικᾶν. πάντας μὲν γὰρ ἁπάντων εἶναι ἀρίστους ἀδύνατον.

1 Cor. IX 25 (ἵνα ... στέφανον λάβωσιν, 2 Tim. II 5, IV 8, Hebr. II 7.9, James I 12, 1 Ptr. V 4, Apoc. passim): Ael. Arist. 2, 418 (45, p. 142) ὁ στέφανος νίκης ἐστὶ σύμβολον. 37, 22 (2, p. 24) τοὺς νικῶντας στεφανοῦν. 5, 45 (29, p. 569) αὐτοὶ δ' ἀγῶνα τοσοῦτον ἀράμενοι καὶ μικροῦ πάντα κατειργασμένοι συγκεκλεικότες Συρακοσίους, ἔχοντες τὴν Σικελίαν μόνον οὐκ ἐν ταῖς χερσί, τὸν στέφανον εἶτα ἀπορρίψομεν; 12, 54 (34, p. 663) ὅμοιον γάρ ἐστι τοῦτό γε ὥσπερ ἂν εἴ τις πυγμὴν ἤ τι τοιοῦτον ἀγωνιζόμενος μέχρι μὲν τῶν ἄθλων ἔλθοι προθύμως, ἔπειτ' ἐξειργασμένων αὐτῷ τῶν πραγμάτων, καί τόν γε στέφανον δέον ἤδη λαμβάνειν τοῖς ἡττωμένοις αὐτὸν προσνείμειεν ἐξαίφνης. Cf. 1, 399. For the agon-motif see V. C. Pfitzner, *Paul and the Agon Motif*, Leiden 1967.

1 Cor. X 13: [Ael. Arist.] 25, 38 (43, p. 811) ἡγοῦμαι δ' ἔγωγε καὶ τὸ τηλικαῦτα ἀτυχεῖν οὐ τοῖς μικροτάτοις τῶν ἀνθρώπων ἀποκεῖσθαι οὐδὲ τοῖς οὐκ ἔχουσιν ὅθεν πέσωσιν, ἀλλὰ τοῖς δυναμένοις δέξασθαι τοῦτο τὸ μέτρον τῆς συμφορᾶς.

1 Cor. X 18.20: Ael. Arist. 45, 27 (8, p. 93-4) καὶ τοίνυν καὶ θυσιῶν μόνῳ τούτῳ θεῷ διαφερόντως κοινωνοῦσιν ἄνθρωποι τὴν ἀκριβῆ κοινωνίαν.

1 Cor. XI 7 (εἰκὼν θεοῦ, 2 Cor. IV 4, Col. I 15, III 10): Ael. Arist. 40, 17 (5, p. 60) ἡ πόλις εἰκών τις 'Ηρακλέους.

1 Cor. XI 14 (ἡ φύσις αὐτὴ διδάσκει): Ael. Arist. 2, 210 (45, p. 39) καὶ λόγων καὶ πραγμάτων ἁπάντων καὶ θεῶν καὶ ἀνθρώπων ἡγεμών ἐστιν φύσις.

I Cor. XI 23 (XV I and 3: παραλαμβάνω as tradition terminology): Ael. Arist. I, 75 (13, p. 186): we have to mention the war-deeds of the Athenians, ἄλλως τε καὶ πλείους μὲν ἢ τὰς τῶν ἄλλων συμπάντων, μείζους δὲ ἁπασῶν οὔσας ὧν παρειλήφαμεν. I, 366 (13, p. 309) δύο τοίνυν ἀνδράσι τῶν πρόσθεν ἐκ θεῶν ψῆφον δεδόσθαι παρειλήφαμεν, Λυκούργῳ τε τῷ Λακεδαιμονίῳ καὶ Σωκράτει τῷ παρ' ὑμῶν.

I Cor. XII and XIV: Ael. Arist. 2, 34-43 (45, pp. 11-13), this whole passage deals with the Pythia and her inspiration, which is perhaps remotely parallel to these chapters of Paul.

I Cor. XII 4-31: Ael. Arist. 2, 321 (45, p. 105) οὐ γὰρ ἦμεν τῆς σῆς ἀρετῆς καὶ σοφίας ἐπιστήμονες, πάντα δ' οὐ πᾶσιν οἱ θεοὶ διδόασιν.

I Cor. XII 11 (τὸ πνεῦμα, διαιροῦν ἰδίᾳ ἑκάστῳ): Ael. Arist. 37, 13 (2, p. 18) Athena τοῖς καθ' ἕκαστα διεῖλέν τε καὶ διαιρεῖ.

I Cor. XIII 1ff.: Ael. Arist. 47, I (23, p. 445) ἀλλ' οὐδ' ἂν εἰ πᾶσαν ὑπερβαλοίμην τὴν ἐν ἀνθρώποις δύναμίν τε καὶ φωνὴν καὶ γνώμην, ...

I Cor. XIII 11 (ἐλάλουν ... ἐφρόνουν): Ael. Arist. 37, 29 (2, p. 28) φρονεῖν καὶ λέγειν.

I Cor. XIII 13 (... τὰ τρία ταῦτα): Ael. Arist. 13, 20 (35, p. 678) ... δόξαν φιλανθρωπίας, μεγαλοψυχίας, ἀνδρείας προσλαβεῖν; ἐν γὰρ τῷ σῶσαι μὴ μνησικακήσαντας τρία ταῦτα ἐστὶν εἰς φιλοτιμίαν τείνοντα.

I Cor. XIV 33: Ael. Arist. 43, 19 (I, p. 7) τὴν τάξιν οὐκ ἀνόνητον ἀξιῶν εἶναι, sc. Zeus.

I Cor. XIV 34ff. (I Tim. II 11ff.): Ael. Arist. 41, 9 (4, p. 50) οὐ τοὺς ἄνδρας θηλύνειν μᾶλλον ἢ τὰς γυναῖκας εἰς ἀνδρῶν τάξιν καθιστάναι Διονυσιακόν. Note the contrast with Paul.

I Cor. XIV 40 (εὐσχημόνως καὶ κατὰ τάξιν): Ael. Arist. 3, 559 (46, p. 364) εἰ δὲ εὐσχημόνως, καὶ τεταγμένως.

I Cor. XV 5 (ὤφθη): Ael. Arist. 51, 22 (27, p. 539) a dream-story is introduced by ὤφθη τοιάδε.

I Cor. XV 5-7: Ael. Arist. 38, 21 (7, p. 78): it is said about the Asclepiads after their death, αὐτοὺς πολλοὶ μὲν ἤδη ἐν Ἐπιδαύρῳ εἶδόν τε καὶ ἔγνωσαν ἐμφανῆ κινουμένους, πολλοὶ δὲ ἄλλοθι πολλαχοῦ.

I Cor. XV 6 (ἐξ ὧν οἱ πλείονες μένουσιν ἕως ἄρτι): Ael. Arist. 9, 30 (38, p. 722) ... καὶ πάνθ' ὅσα τοιαῦτα, ἐάσομεν. ἀλλ' ὧν ἔτι ζῶσιν οἱ μάρτυρες, τοῦτο μὲν ...

I Cor. XV 28: Ael. Arist. 50, 108 (26, p. 533) πάντα ... ὑπεχώρει τῷ θεῷ.

I Cor. XV 57 (τῷ θεῷ ... τῷ διδόντι ἡμῖν τὸ νῖκος): Ael. Arist. 43, 30 (I, p. II) Ζεὺς ... νίκην διδούς. 37, 27 (2, p. 27) Ἀθηνᾶ ... τὴν νίκην ἑκάστῳ διδοῦσα.

I Cor. XVI 17 (ὑστέρημα ἀνεπλήρωσαν): Ael. Arist. 2, 418 (45, p. 142) τὰ ἐλαττώματα ἀναπληροῖ.

I Cor. XVI 21 (τῇ ἐμῇ χειρί, Gal. VI II, Col. IV 18, 2 Thess. III 17, Philemon 19): Ael. Arist. 48, 2 (24, p. 465) ἐγὼ δὲ τῶν ὀνειράτων τὴν ἀπογραφὴν ἐποιούμην, ὁπότε μὴ δυναίμην αὐτοχειρίᾳ, ὑπαγορεύων γε (dictating).

2 CORINTHIANS

2 Cor. I 3-7 (God's παράκλησις (= παραμυθία), VII 4-7, 2 Thess. II 17): Ael. Arist. 48, 25 (24, p. 472) παρὰ τοῦ θεοῦ ... παραμυθίαι παντοῖαι. 48, 42 (24, p. 476) ἡ θεὸς ... παρεμυθήσατο.

2 Cor. I 10 (ἐκ τηλικούτου θανάτου ἐρρύσατο ἡμᾶς, sc. God; cf. 2 Tim. III 11, IV 17, Hebr. V 7): Ael. Arist. 49, 4 (25, p. 489) πολλοὺς δ' ἐκ θανάτοιο ἐρύσατο, sc. the God (this is a quotation from a song composed by Aristides).

2 Cor. III 16-17a ("ἐὰν ἐπιστρέψῃ πρὸς κύριον, ..." (Ex. XXXIV 34). ὁ δὲ κύριος τὸ πνεῦμά ἐστιν): Ael. Arist. 2, 389f. (45, p. 131) "ἀσφαλῶς ἀγορεύει", φησίν (sc. Homer in *Od.* VIII 171). τὸ δὲ ἀσφαλῶς ἔστιν ἀπταίστως.

2 Cor. IV 7 (ἡ ὑπερβολὴ τῆς δυνάμεως, cf. Eph. I 19): Ael. Arist. 37, 22 (2, p. 24) ἡ δὲ ὑπερβολὴ τοῦ κράτους.

2 Cor. V 4 + 8 (?): Ael. Arist. 38, 20 (7, p. 78) ... ἀποδύντες τὰ σώματα εἰς ἕτερον θεσμὸν ἔρχονται, sc. to heaven.

2 Cor. VI 2 (Hebr. IV 16, God's βοήθεια): Ael. Arist. 47, 72 (23, p. 463) γενομένης γε κἀμοὶ παρὰ τοῦ θεοῦ βοηθείας.

2 Cor. VI 6 ("Tugendkatalog"): Ael. Arist. 1, 154 (13, p. 226) ... πάντων ὅσα<ἄν>τις εἴποι μέγιστα κατ' ἀνθρώπους ἐν ἡμέρᾳ μιᾷ παρασχόμενοι σύμβολα εὐσεβείας, καρτερίας, φρονήσεως, φιλανθρωπίας, μεγαλοψυχίας. All these virtues also occur in early Christian literature (references can easily be found in Bauer's *Wörterbuch*), except μεγαλοψυχία (on which see R. A. Gauthier, *Magnanimité*, Paris 1951). Cf. 37, 27 (2, p. 27) φρόνησις δὲ καὶ σωφροσύνη καὶ ἀνδρεία καὶ ὁμόνοια καὶ εὐταξία καὶ εὐπραγία.

2 Cor. VI 14 (τίς κοινωνία φωτὶ πρὸς σκότος; κοινωνία occurs passim in the N.T., κοινωνία πρός + acc. only here): Ael. Arist. 37, 21 (2, p. 22) ἥ γε πρὸς Ἑρμῆν κοινωνία τῆς θεοῦ (sc. Athena).

2 Cor. VI 15 (τίς δὲ συμφώνησις Χριστοῦ πρὸς Βελιάρ;): Ael. Arist. 37, 20 (2, p. 22) τὴν Ἀσκληπιοῦ καὶ Ἀθηνᾶς συμφωνίαν.

2 Cor. VIII 22 (ἐν πολλοῖς πολλάκις): Ael. Arist. 1, 7 (13, p. 154) ὑπο πολλῶν πολλάκις. 1, 248 (13, p. 269) πολλὰ δὴ πολλάκις. 38, 4 (7, p. 72) ὦ πολλὰ δὴ πολλάκις κληθείς. Cf. also 42, 1 (6, p. 63) and 38, 21 (7, p. 78).

2 Cor. IX 15 (τῇ ἀνεκδιηγήτῳ αὐτοῦ (sc. θεοῦ) δωρεᾷ): Ael. Arist. 45, 16 (8, p. 88) ἐμοὶ δὲ τὰ τοῦ μεγίστου τῶν θεῶν ἔργα τε καὶ δῶρα εἰς ἀνθρώπους ἀεὶ τελούμενα ἢ που σφόδρα ἀμήχανον ἁπάντων ἀνθρώπων στόματα καὶ πᾶσαν ὅση ἀνθρωπίνη φωνὴ κτησαμένῳ, εἰ μὴ θεοί τινες ὡς ἀληθῶς ἡγεμόνες τῷ λόγῳ γένοιντο. 47, 1 (23, p. 445) ἀλλ' οὐδ' ἂν εἰ πᾶσαν ὑπερβαλοίμην τὴν ἐν ἀνθρώποις δύναμίν τε καὶ φωνὴν καὶ γνώμην, οὐκ ἄν ποτε οὐδ' ἐγγὺς αὐτῶν (sc. τῶν τοῦ Σωτῆρος ἀγωνισμάτων) ἀφικοίμην.

2 Cor. X 1 (διὰ τῆς πραΰτητος καὶ ἐπιεικείας τοῦ Χριστοῦ, Tit. III 2 ἐπιεικεῖς, πᾶσαν ἐνδεικνυμένους πραΰτητα): Ael. Arist. 1, 8 (13, p. 155) (on the Athenians) ἐναργῆ καὶ θαυμαστὰ τῆς αὐτῶν ἐπιεικείας σημεῖα ἐξήνεγκαν ἐν παντὶ τῷ παρασχόντι .... φιλανθρωπίαν ἐπιδεικνύμενοι τῇ τῶν τρόπων πραότητι. Cf. ibid. 136 (p. 217) where ἐπιείκεια and πραότης are also mentioned as characteristics of Athens. Cf. also 38, 24 (7, p. 80) on the πραότης of the Asclepiads, and 35, 22 (9, p. 106) on the ἐπιείκεια of the emperor.

2 Cor. XI 22-23 (only a stylistic parallel): Ael. Arist. 3, 115 (46, p. 198) λάλους, φησίν, ἐποίησε· καὶ μὴν οὐκ ἦν αὐτὸς λάλος. ἀργούς· ὁ δ' ἐνεργὸς ἦν. δειλούς· ὁ δὲ νικῶν ἀνδρείᾳ φαίνεται. φιλοχρημάτους· ὁ δ' ἥκιστα ἐτίμα χρήματα.

2 Cor. XI 26 (κινδύνοις ἐν θαλάσσῃ): Ael. Arist. 43, 2 (1, p. 1) ἀλλὰ νῦν μοι δοκῶ καὶ σφόδρα μανθάνειν ὡς τελέως ἄρα ἐκινδύνευον, καὶ οὐκ ἐν ἐμαυτῷ ἦν ὑπὸ τῆς θαλάττης.

2 Cor. XII 1-4 (esp. v. 4 ἄρρητα ῥήματα): Ael. Arist. 49, 48 (25, p. 501) ... ἕτερα ἔκπληξιν θαυμαστὴν φέροντα, καὶ οὐδὲ ῥητὰ ἴσως εἰς ἅπαντας,... κεφάλαιον δ' ἦν περὶ τῆς τοῦ θεοῦ δυνάμεως, ὅτι καὶ χωρὶς ὀχημάτων καὶ χωρὶς σωμάτων ὁ Σάραπις οἷός τ' εἴη κομίζειν ἀνθρώπους ὅπη βούλοιτο. 48, 23 (24, p. 471) οὔτε γὰρ οἷον ἡδονὴ περιφανὴς ἦν οὔτε κατ' ἀνθρωπίνην εὐφροσύνην ἔφησθα ἂν εἶναι αὐτό, ἀλλ' ἦν τις ἄρρητος εὐθυμία, πάντα δεύτερα τοῦ παρόντος καιροῦ τιθεμένη, ὥστε οὐδ' ὁρῶν τὰ ἄλλα ἐδόκουν ὁρᾶν. οὕτω πᾶς ἦν πρὸς τῷ θεῷ. 1, 341 (13, p. 302) τὰς δ' ἀρρήτους τελετάς, ὧν τοῖς μετασχοῦσι καὶ μετὰ τὴν τοῦ βίου τελευτὴν βελτίω τὰ πράγματα γίγνεσθαι δοκεῖ (sc. the

mysteries of Eleusis). Cf. also on the Eleusinian mysteries 22, 3 (19, p. 416) τοῖς ἀρρήτοις φάσμασιν. 45, 32 (8, p. 96) Sarapis is φύλαξ τῶν φανερῶν καὶ τῶν ἀπορρήτων. 49, 46 (25, p. 500) ἐγένετο δὲ καὶ φῶς παρὰ τῆς Ἴσιδος καὶ ἕτερα ἀμύθητα φέροντα εἰς σωτηρίαν.

GALATIANS

Gal. I 4 (Christ's διδόναι ἑαυτόν, 1 Tim. II 6, Tit. II 14): Ael. Arist. 46, 9 (3, p. 32) Poseidon δοὺς ἑαυτὸν εἰς ἅπαντα τῷ γένει τῶν ἀνθρώπων.

Gal. I 16 (μετατίθεσθαι, cf. ἀμετάθετος in Hebr. VI 17-8): Ael. Arist. 1, 158 (13, p. 227) οὕτω γὰρ πόρρω δέους ἢ τοῦ μεταθέσθαι περὶ τῶν ἐξ ἀρχῆς ἐγνωσμένων ἐγένοντο ὥστε κτλ.

Gal. II 2 (ἀνέβην (sc. to Jerusalem) δὲ κατὰ ἀποκάλυψιν): Ael. Arist. 49, 43 (25, p. 499) ... ἐπανιὼν εἰς τὴν πόλιν ἐξ ἐνυπνίων.

Gal. II 8 (God gives strength, Phil. IV 13, 1 Tim. I 12, 2 Tim. IV 17): Ael. Arist. 50, 17 (26, p. 506) δυνάμεως δὲ μελήσει τῷ θεῷ.

Gal. III 8 (προϊδοῦσα δὲ ἡ γραφή): Ael. Arist. 1, 329 (13, p. 296) ὥσπερ γὰρ προειδυῖα ἐξ ἀρχῆς ἡ φύσις κτλ. This is about fore-knowledge of non-human entities, but see also *ad* Acts II 31.

Gal. III 17: Ael. Arist. 45, 8 (8, p. 85) τὸ πρότερον καὶ πρεσβύτερον καὶ κατ' αὐτοὺς ἄμεινον τοὺς ποιητάς.

Gal. IV 9 (..., οἷς πάλιν ἄνωθεν δουλεύειν θέλετε;): Ael. Arist. 6, 33 (30, p. 582) οὐδεὶς γὰρ ἑκὼν οἶμαι δουλεύειν βούλεται.

Gal. IV 18 (καλὸν δὲ ζηλοῦσθαι ἐν καλῷ, cf. 1 Tim. III 13, Hebr. XIII 18): Ael. Arist. 26, 105 (14, p. 367) αὐτῷ (sc. Zeus) τῆς οἰκουμένης καλοῦ, φασίν, ἔργου καλῶς ἐπιμέλεσθε.

Gal. IV 26 ('Ιερουσαλὴμ ... ἥτις ἐστὶν μήτηρ ἡμῶν, cf. Apoc. XVII 5): Ael. Arist. 30, 4 (10, p. 115) ... μητέρα τὴν πόλιν ἐξεῖναι καλεῖν.

Gal. V 1 (Χριστὸς ἠλευθέρωσεν): Ael. Arist. 43, 30 (1, p. 11) (on Zeus) οὗτος 'Ελευθέριος.

Gal. VI 12 (εὐπροσωπῆσαι): Ael. Arist. 12, 8 (34, p. 644) ἴστε γὰρ δή που τοῦθ' ὅτι οὐδέν ἐστιν εὐπροσωπότερον Λακεδαιμονίων πλεονεκτεῖν ζητούντων.

Eph. I 6 (ἔπαινος of God, I 12 and 14, Phil. I 11): Ael. Arist. 40, 1 (5, p. 53) ὁ καθ' ἡμέραν ὑπὸ πάντων ἔπαινος (sc. of Heracles) ἐπὶ πάσης τῆς παραπιπτούσης προφάσεως ἀιεὶ γιγνόμενος. 42, 13 (6, p. 69) τὸν ἔπαινον ἐκτείνων ... σοῦ τοῦ κυρίου (sc. Asclepius).

Eph. I 8 (ἐν πάσῃ σοφίᾳ καὶ φρονήσει): [Ael. Arist.] 35, 33 (9, p. 110) ..., φρονήσει δὲ καί σοφίᾳ κρατεῖν δύνασθαι μόνων ἐστὶ τῶν εἰδότων βουλεύεσθαι.

Eph. I 16 (οὐ παύομαι εὐχαριστῶν): Ael. Arist. 42, 15 (6, p. 70) τὴν δυνατὴν ἔχοντες χάριν οὐ παυσόμεθα.

Eph. I 19 (God's ἰσχύς, VI 10, 2 Thess. I 9; cf. Apoc. XVIII 8): Ael. Arist. 46, 37 (3, p. 45) (Λευκοθέα) ... οὐδ' ἂν ἔσχεν ἰσχὺν τοσαύτην ὅσην ἀκούομεν (see the whole context).

Eph. I 23b (τοῦ τὰ πάντα ἐν πᾶσιν πληρουμένου, IV 10 ἵνα πληρώσῃ τὰ πάντα): Ael. Arist. 45, 21 (8, p. 91) Sarapis διὰ πάντων ἥκει καὶ τὸ πᾶν πεπλήρωκε. Cf. 43, 26 (1, p. 10) πάντα δὲ πανταχοῦ Διὸς μεστά.

Eph. II 2 (τὸν ἄρχοντα τῆς ἐξουσίας τοῦ ἀέρος): Ael. Arist. 43, 18 (1, p. 7) καὶ τοῖς μέν γε δὴ θεοῖς τὰς τέτταρας ἀπέδωκεν χώρας, ὅπως μηδαμοῦ μηδὲν κενὸν εἴη θεῶν, ἀλλὰ πανταχοῦ πᾶσι παρεῖεν, οὖσί τε καὶ γιγνομένοις, τὴν δὴ πατρίδα τὴν οὐράνιον καὶ τὴν κατ' ἀ έ ρ α καὶ τὴν ἐν θαλάττῃ καὶ τὴν ἐπὶ γῆς οἷον ὕπαρχοί τινες καὶ σατράπαι μεμερισμένοι.

Eph. II 3 (τέκνα φύσει ὀργῆς): Ael. Arist. 1, 281 (13, p. 279) τοὺς βαρβάρους τοὺς φύσει πολεμίους. 37, 9 (2, p. 15) (τοὺς Γίγαντας) ... φύσει πολεμίους ὄντας.

Eph. II 8 (θεοῦ τὸ δῶρον, cf. John IV 10, Acts VIII 20): Ael. Arist. 1, 44 (13, p. 170) ταῖς γὰρ τιμαῖς τῶν θεῶν ἠκολούθει τὰ δῶρα διδόντων καὶ λαμβανόντων ἐκ τῶν αὐτῶν τὰ ἐπιβάλλοντα ἑκατέροις. 37, 13 (2, p. 17) δῶρα 'Αθηνᾶς.

Eph. II 12 (ἐλπίδα μὴ ἔχοντες καὶ ἄθεοι ἐν τῷ κόσμῳ): Ael. Arist. 45, 18 (8, p. 89) ἀνθρώπων δὲ οὓς ἂν προλίπῃ (sc. Sarapis) ζῶντες οἰκτείρονται μᾶλλον ἢ τελευτήσαντες.

Eph. II 14 (ἀμφότερα, neuter plural, for two kinds or groups of people): Ael. Arist. 41, 3 (4, p. 47) ὁ Ζεὺς βουλόμενος ἀμφότερα αὐτὸς τῷ Διονύσῳ γενέσθαι, πατήρ τε καὶ μήτηρ.

Eph. II 19 (συμπολῖται τῶν ἁγίων καὶ οἰκεῖοι τοῦ θεοῦ, cf. Phil. III 20): Ael. Arist. 46, 9 (3, p. 32) (Ποσειδῶν) παρέχων ἑαυτῷ ... συμπολιτεύεσθαι.

Eph. III 10 (VI 12, Col. I 16, II 10 and 15, 1 Ptr. III 22: ἐξουσίαι, θρόνοι, ἀρχαί, κυριότητες): Ael. Arist. 43, 18 (1, p. 7) οἷον ὕπαρχοί τινες καὶ σατράπαι (for the whole passage see *ad* Eph. II 2).

Eph. III 12 (ἔχομεν τὴν παρρησίαν καὶ προσαγωγὴν ἐν πεποιθήσει, cf. Hebr. IV 16, X 19): Ael. Arist. 46, 11 (3, p. 32) ἀνεῖπεν οὗτος ὁ θεὸς (sc. Poseidon) φοιτᾶν παρ' ἑαυτὸν θαρρούντως.

Eph. III 17 (ἐν ἀγάπῃ ἐρριζωμένοι καὶ τεθεμελιωμένοι, cf. Col. II 7): Ael. Arist. 43, 11 (1, p. 4) ἄρχεται ἐκ θεμελίων ... ῥιζώσας ... πυκνώσας κτλ.

Eph. III 20 (δυναμένῳ ... ποιῆσαι ὑπερεκπερισσοῦ ὧν αἰτούμεθα ἢ νοοῦμεν): Ael. Arist. 43, 13 (1, p. 5) Zeus ἀποτελεώσας ἅπαντα ... ὀξύτερον ἢ νοῆσα, ἐγχωρεῖ. Cf. 1, 92 (13, p. 195) ... τότ' ἐνίκησεν ἡ πόλις ἄμφω τὼ γένη κάλλιον εὐχῆς.

Eph. IV 3 (σύνδεσμος metaphorically used): Ael. Arist. 5, 39 (29, p. 566) σύνδεσμος ... τῆς ἀρχῆς καθεστήξει.

Eph. IV 6 (εἷς θεὸς καὶ πατὴρ πάντων): Ael. Arist. 43, 15 (1, p. 6) Διὸς τοῦ πάντων πατρός. ibid. 29 (p. 10) Ζεὺς πάντων πατήρ. Cf. ibid. 6 (p. 2) τὸν ... τῶν ὅλων πατέρα. See also 44, 11 (17, p. 404) and 37, 2 (2, p. 13).

Eph. IV 9 (τὰ κατώτερα μέρη τῆς γῆς): Ael. Arist. 46, 5 (3, p. 31) τῆς κάτω μοίρας = the earth.

Eph. IV 27 (μηδὲ δίδοτε τόπον τῷ διαβόλῳ): Ael. Arist. 24, 37 (44, p. 836) οὐ δώσει χώραν τοῖς παροξυσμοῖς.

Eph. V 1 (γίνεσθε οὖν μιμηταὶ τοῦ θεοῦ, cf. 1 Thess. I 6): Ael. Arist. 43, 28 (1, p. 10) μιμούμενος τὸν πατέρα, sc. Δία. 23, 77 (42, p. 794) τὸ μιμεῖσθαι τοὺς κρείττους (the gods) εὖ φρονούντων ἐστίν. 46, 14 (3, p. 34) κατὰ τὴν πρὸς Δία μίμησιν. 1, 34 (13, p. 166) λαβόντες δὲ οὕτω τὰς παρὰ τῶν θεῶν δωρεὰς οὕτως εὖ τοὺς δόντας ἐμιμήσαντο ὥστε αὐτοὶ τοῖς ἄλλοις ἀνθρώποις ἀντὶ τῶν θεῶν κατέστησαν. 36, 123 (48,

p. 488) ... τοῦ θεοῦ, ὅστις ᾗ μὲν ἥκιστα ὕειν ἔμελλεν, τὸν Νεῖλον ἐπήγαγεν μιμητήν τινα ἑαυτοῦ καὶ ἀντὶ ὄμβρων εἶναι τοῖς ταύτῃ. Cf. also 39, 11 (18, p. 412).

Eph. V 19 (λαλοῦντες ... ὕμνοις..., αἴδοντες ... τῷ κυρίῳ, Col. III 16): Ael. Arist. 43, 2 (1, p. 1) ὕμνον ἐρεῖν Διός (to recite a prose-hymn for Zeus. For the diction cf. Plinius Minor, *Epist.* X 96 *carmen Christo quasi deo dicere.* On ὕμνος see M. P. Nilsson, *Gesch. der griech. Relig.* II² 377ff.). Cf. 40, 1 (5, p. 53) ᾄδοντες τὰ σά.

Eph. V 26 (Tit. III 5, λουτρόν for a ritual and sacral bath): Ael. Arist. 48, 71 (24, p. 484) a comparable use of λουτρόν.

Eph. VI 1-9 (Col. III 20-IV 1): Ael. Arist. 24, 33 (44, p. 834/5) εἰσὶν ἄρχοντες ἐν οἰκίᾳ πατέρες παίδων καὶ δούλων δεσπόται. πῶς οὖν οὗτοι καλῶς οἰκοῦσιν; ὅταν οἱ μὲν ἄρχοντες μὴ πάντ' ἐξεῖναι νομίζωσιν ἑαυτοῖς, ἀλλ' ἑκόντες ὑφαιρῶσι τῆς ἐξουσίας, οἱ δ' ὅτι ἂν δοκῇ τοῖς κρείττοσιν ὡς ἐξὸν δέχωνται. ἄνευ δὲ ταύτης τῆς ἑκατέρωθεν εὐγνωμοσύνης οὐ ῥᾴδιον εὑρεῖν οἰκίαν ἥτις σωθήσεται.

Eph. VI 5ff.: Ael. Arist. 2, 128 (45, p. 40) δεσπότης δ' οἰκέτου τῷ διαφέρει ...; οὐ δεσπότου μὲν προστάξαι, δούλου δ' ὑπακοῦσαι πᾶς τις ἂν φήσειεν εἶναι;

PHILIPPIANS

Phil. I 3-4 (alliteration with the π in ... ἐπὶ πάσῃ τῇ μνείᾳ ὑμῶν, πάντοτε ἐν πάσῃ δεήσει μου ὑπὲρ πάντων ὑμῶν μετὰ χαρᾶς τὴν δέησιν ποιούμενος, ἐπὶ κτλ.): Ael. Arist. 1, 45 (13, p. 170) ... ἐν τῇδε τῇ πόλει τὰς κρίσεις ἐποιήσαντο, πανταχόθεν πάντας ἀνθρώπους ἐπιστρέφοντες πρὸς τὴν πόλιν καὶ πάντων ἀρχὰς ... 1, 73 (13, p. 185) καὶ μὴν δεξάμενοι τοὺς ἁπανταχόθεν, πανταχῇ καὶ πεπόμφασι, ...

Phil. I 6 (ὁ ἐναρξάμενος ἐν ὑμῖν ἔργον ἀγαθόν) Ael. Arist. 46, 36 (3, p. 44) ἀγαθὰ δὲ ἔργα τὰ θεῶν. Cf. James I 17.

Phil. I 21 (κέρδος, III 7): Ael. Arist. 51, 56 (27, p. 548) ἔτι δὲ οὐδ' ἀπόρως εἶχον ἐμαυτῷ συνεῖναι, ἀλλὰ καὶ κέρδος αὐτὸ μᾶλλον ἐποιούμην.

Phil. I 23 (σὺν Χριστῷ εἶναι, 1 Thess. IV 17 σὺν κυρίῳ ἐσόμεθα, said of life after death): Ael. Arist. 50, 52 (26, p. 518) συνεῖναι θεῷ ... συγγενέσθαι θεῷ, said of Aristides' contact with the god by means of his dreams.

Phil. II 6 (ἴσα θεῷ): Ael. Arist. 37, 2 (2, p. 13) the goddess Athena is ἐξ ἴσου καὶ ὁμολογοῦντος ἑαυτῷ (sc. Διὶ) τοῦ γένους γενομένη.

Phil. II 7 (μορφὴν δούλου λαβών): Ael. Arist. 2, 224 (45, p. 68) ἐκείνη (sc. νομοθετικῇ) τε γὰρ ῥητορικῆς πρότερον ἐδέησεν, ὥστε ταύτῃ ἔχειν πάροδον <ἐπὶ> τοὺς νόμους, ἥ τε δικαστικὴ σχῆμα ἐπικούρου λαβοῦσα τοῖς νόμοις αὐτὴ πρότερον προσεδεήθη τῆς παρὰ τῆς ῥητορικῆς βοηθείας.

Phil. II 7-8 (σχήματι εὑρεθεὶς ὡς ἄνθρωπος ἐταπείνωσεν ἑαυτόν): Ael. Arist. 13, 16 (35, p. 676) ... φύγοιεν ἄν, οἶμαι, ταπεινὸν οὕτω σχῆμα λαβεῖν, ὥστ' ἐπὶ τὸν βάρβαρον καὶ κηλῖδα παλαιὰν ἐπανελθεῖν.

Phil. II 10 (ἐπουρανίων καὶ ἐπιγείων καὶ καταχθονίων, cf. 1 Cor. XV 40): Ael. Arist. 43, 23 (1, p. 9) ὅσα τε οὐράνια καὶ ὅσα ἐπίγεια. Cf. ibid. 7 (p. 2) καὶ γῆ ... καὶ οὐρανὸς καὶ ὅσα τούτων μεταξὺ καὶ ὅσα ἄνω καὶ ὅσα ὑπὸ ταῦτα (for this reading see J. Amann, *Die Zeusrede des Ailios Aristeides*, Stuttgart 1931, 38).

Phil. II 13: Ael. Arist. 50, 51 (26, p. 518) the God honoured me, and τοῦτ' ἐμὲ καὶ δύνασθαι καὶ βούλεσθαι ζῆν ἐποίησεν.

Phil. III 7: Ael. Arist. 6, 46 (30, p. 587) ... φημί τιν' ἡμῶν κέρδος τὴν ζημίαν ἡγήσεσθαι. 28, 100 (49, p. 524) οὐ γὰρ δή που σὺ μὲν ζημίαν ποιῇ ἐμοῦ τοῖς ἐμαυτοῦ χαίροντος, ἐγὼ δ' οὐ ποιήσομαι κέρδος, ἂν σὺ λυπῇ διὰ ταῦτα. 33, 30 (51, p. 581) πάντα μὲν τὰ αἴσχιστα ἐν κέρδους τάξει τιθέμενος, πᾶν δ' ὅσον χρηστὸν ζημίαν καὶ πόνους ἄλλως ὑπολαμβάνων.

Phil. III 12 (κατελήμφθην ὑπὸ Χριστοῦ): Ael. Arist. 50, 4 (26, p. 503) ἐνταῦθα δὴ παντελῶς οἱονεὶ καθιερώμην τε καὶ εἰχόμην (sc. ὑπὸ τοῦ Σωτῆρος), καί μοι πολλὰ μὲν εἰς αὐτὸν τὸν Σωτῆρα ἐποιήθη μέλη.

Phil. IV 3 (γνήσιος, for friends and children, 1 Tim. I 2, Tit. I 4): Ael. Arist. 2, 76 (45, p. 24) ἀλλ' εἴ γέ τινας ὥσπερ παῖδας οὕτως καὶ ἑταίρους χρὴ λέγειν γνησίους, γνήσιον Αἰσχίνην Σωκράτους παρειλήφαμεν.

Phil. IV 7 (ἡ εἰρήνη τοῦ θεοῦ ἡ ὑπερέχουσα πάντα νοῦν): Ael. Arist. 48, 49 (24, p. 478) ἡ δὲ ἐπὶ τούτῳ κουφότης καὶ ἀναψυχὴ θεῷ μὲν καὶ μάλα ῥᾳδία γνῶναι, ἀνθρώπῳ δὲ ἢ νῷ λαβεῖν ἢ ἐνδείξασθαι λόγῳ οὐ πάνυ ῥᾴδιον.

Phil. IV 19a: Ael. Arist. 39, 11 (10, p. 412) the well of Asclepius αἰεὶ πληροῖ τὴν τῶν δεομένων χρείαν.

COLOSSIANS

Col. I 15-20: Ael. Arist. 43, 7 (1, p. 2) Ζεὺς τὰ πάντα ἐποίησεν καὶ Διός ἐστιν ἔργα ὅσα ἐστὶ πάντα, καὶ ποταμοὶ καὶ γῆ καὶ θάλαττα καὶ οὐρανὸς καὶ ὅσα τούτων μεταξὺ καὶ ὅσα ὑπὲρ ταῦτα, καὶ θεοὶ καὶ ἄνθρωποι καὶ ὅσα ψυχὴν ἔχει καὶ ὅσα εἰς ὄψιν ἀφικνεῖται καὶ ὅσα δεῖ νοήσει λαβεῖν (note in Col. I 16 τὰ ὁρατὰ καὶ τὰ ἀόρατα). See the remarks of W. Pöhlmann, Die hymnischen All-Prädikationen in Kol. I 15-20, *ZNW* 64 (1973), 53-74, esp. 60. Cf. also 43, 29 (1, p. 10-11).

Col. II 11 (τῇ ἀπεκδύσει τοῦ σώματος): Ael. Arist. 38, 20 (7, p. 78) (on the Asclepiads) ἐπεὶ δὲ κρείττους ἦσαν ἢ παρ' ἡμῖν μένειν, οἱ δὲ ὑπὸ τοῦ πατρός τε καὶ τῶν προγόνων ἀποδύντες τὰ σώματα εἰς ἕτερον θεσμὸν ἔρχονται.

Col. III 8-9 (ἀπόθεσθε ... ὀργήν, θυμόν, κτλ ... ἀπεκδυσάμενοι τὸν παλαιὸν ἄνθρωπον): Ael. Arist. 16, 41 (52, p. 608) ἐκδὺς τὴν ὀργὴν ὥσπερ νόσον φάνηθι τοῖς βαρβάροις ἅμα τῷ ἡλίῳ (said to Achilles who cherishes his wrath).

Col. III 11 (οὐκ ἔνι Ἕλλην καὶ Ἰουδαῖος, ..., βάρβαρος, Σκύθης, κτλ.): Ael. Arist. 9, 44 (38, p. 728-9) ... Φίλιππον μὲν αἱρούμενοι, βάρβαρον ἄνθρωπον καὶ φύσει κεχωρισμένον αἱρεῖσθε (note the equivalence of βάρβαρος and φύσει κεχωρισμένος, in antithesis to Col. III 11). 1, 15 (13, p. 158) the city of Athens τοσοῦτον δὲ πέφευγε τὴν ἀλλοδαπῆ καὶ βάρβαρον, ὥστε καὶ ἐπὶ τῆς ἀντιπέρας ἠπείρου προὐβάλλετο ἑτέραν Ἑλλάδα ἄποικον ἑαυτῆς (sc. Ionia), ἣ νῦν ἤδη πλεῖστον βαρβάρων ἀφέστηκεν, ὥσπερ φύσει ταχθεῖσα ἡ πόλις, ἀντίπαλος τούτῳ τῷ γένει καὶ πολεμία.

Col. IV 5 (πρὸς τοὺς ἔξω, 1 Thess. IV 12): Ael. Arist. 34, 8 (50, p. 548) ... πρὸς δὲ τοὺς ἔξω σχηματίζεσθαι. 6, 9 (30, p. 573) τὰ ψηφίσματα καὶ τὰς γνώμας οἱ καιροὶ καὶ ποιοῦσι καὶ λύουσιν· εἰκότως. ἐν ἐκείνῳ μὲν γὰρ τῷ τρόπῳ τοῖς πολίταις διαλεγόμεθα, ὥστ' ἀρκεῖ φθέγγεσθαι ταὐτὸν διὰ τέλους, ταῦτα δὲ πρὸς τοὺς ἔξω καὶ πρὸς τὰς τοῦ πολέμου τύχας ἀνεύρηται.

Col. IV 16 (ὅταν ἀναγνωσθῇ παρ' ὑμῖν ἡ ἐπιστολή, 1 Thess. V 27): Ael. Arist. 6, 34 (30, p. 582) οὐκ ἀκούετε τῆς ἐπιστολῆς ...;

1 + 2 THESSALONIANS

1 Thess. II 5 (οὔτε ... ἐν λόγῳ κολακείας ἐγενήθημεν): Ael. Arist. 2, 323 (45, p. 106) τί οὖν ἡμῖν προφέρεις κολακείαν καὶ διακονίαν ...; (why do you charge us with flattery and servitude?). ibid. 328 (p. 108) κόλακας καὶ διακόνους καὶ τοῦ μηδενὸς ἀξίους. Note the pejorative use of διακονία and διάκονος.

1 Thess. II 7 (... ὡς ἐὰν τροφὸς θάλπῃ τὰ ἑαυτῆς τέκνα): Ael. Arist. 1, 315 (13, p. 292) πάντων δέ, ὥσπερ μήτηρ ὑπὲρ παίδων, προὔκαμε, sc. the city of Athens.

1 Thess. II 10 (ὅσιος καὶ δίκαιος, Tit. I 8, Apoc. XVI 5): [Ael. Arist.] 35, 14 (9, p. 102) τὸν δικαιότατον καὶ ὁσιώτατον βασιλέων.

1 Thess. III 2 (συνεργὸς τοῦ θεοῦ, *variae lectiones* διάκονος τοῦ θεοῦ and διάκονος καὶ συνεργὸς τοῦ θεοῦ): Ael. Arist. 39, 11 (18, p. 411) διάκονόν τε καὶ συνεργὸν τοῦ φιλανθρωποτάτου τῶν θεῶν.

1 Thess. IV 9 (θεοδίδακτοί ἐστε): Ael. Arist. 42, 4 (6, p. 64) ... ἐμοὶ σαφὴς ὁ διδάσκαλος (sc. Asclepius) ... ταῦτ' ἐδίδαξεν.

1 Thess. V 12 (εἰδέναι in the sense of "to recognize, to honour"; this is the only instance of this sense mentioned by Bauer): [Ael. Arist.] 35, 35 (9, p. 111) πεπαίδευται τοὺς κρείττους εἰδέναι.

2 Thess. I 3 (εὐχαριστεῖν ὀφείλομεν τῷ θεῷ): Ael. Arist. 43, 19 (1, p. 7) μεγάλην μεγάλων ὀφείλοντες χάριν, sc. τῷ Διί.

1 TIMOTHY

1 Tim. I 4 (μηδὲ προσέχειν μύθοις, IV 7, Tit. I 14, 2 Ptr. I 16; the word μῦθος is used always in a negative sense in the N.T.): Ael. Arist. 37, 11 (2, p. 16) τοὺς μύθους μὴ ἀτιμάσαι (here positive). 37, 27 (2, p. 27) δεῖ καταλύσαντα τοὺς μύθους εἰπεῖν εἰς τὸ μέσον τὰ τῆς θεοῦ. 48, 42 (24, p. 476) οὐ μύθους εἶναι ταῦτα, sc. the Odyssee (here negative).

1 Tim. I 9: Ael. Arist. 2, 212 (45, p. 65) ἀλλὰ μὴν τοῦτό γε πάντες ἂν εἴποιεν, ὡς οὐδὲ πρὸς ἓν τῶν πάντων ἐδέησεν νόμων ἡμῖν, ἢ τὸ μηδὲν ὑπ' ἀλλήλων πάσχειν δυσχερές, μηδὲ τοὺς φαύλους καὶ θρασεῖς τῶν χρηστῶν κρατεῖν, ἀλλὰ τοὺς χρηστοὺς τῶν φαύλων περιεῖναι μετὰ τοῦ δικαίου. On βέβηλος cf. 17, 18 (15, p. 380) εἰς ἑτέρους δὲ οὐκ ἂν ῥᾳδίως [τοὺς λόγους] ἐκφέρειν ὥσπερ εἰς βεβήλους τὰ ἱερά.

1 Tim. I 16 (ἐν ἐμοὶ πρώτῳ): Ael. Arist. 37, 29 (2, p. 28) ἐν αὐτῷ δ' ἐμοὶ πρώτῳ.

1 Tim. I 17 (God as βασιλεύς, VI 15, Apoc. XV 3): Ael. Arist. 43, 1 (1, p. 1) Ζεῦ βασιλεῦ. Cf. 30 (p. 11).

1 Tim. II 1-2: Ael. Arist. 46, 42 (3, p. 46) λοιπὸν οὖν εὐξαμένους τῷ Ποσειδῶνι καὶ τῇ Ἀμφιτρίτῃ καὶ τῇ Λευκοθέᾳ καὶ τῷ Παλαίμονι καὶ Νηρηίσι καὶ δαίμοσι θαλαττίοις πᾶσί τε καὶ πάσαις ἀσφάλειάν τε καὶ σωτηρίαν ἔν τε γῇ καὶ ἐν θαλάττῃ διδόναι βασιλεῖ τε τῷ μεγάλῳ καὶ γένει ξύμπαντι τούτου καὶ τῷ γένει τῷ τῶν Ἑλλήνων καὶ κατὰ τὰ ἄλλα τε εὐθενεῖν ἡμᾶς καὶ κατὰ τοὺς λόγους, χωρεῖν ἐπὶ τὰ προσήκοντα ἡμῶν ἑκάστῳ. 26, 109 (14, p. 370) (οἱ θεοὶ ...) διδόντων ... ἄρχοντά τε τὸν μέγαν καὶ παῖδας τούτου σῶς τε εἶναι καὶ πρυτανεύειν πᾶσι τὰ ἀγαθά.

1 Tim. II 4a ((θεοῦ) ὃς πάντας ἀνθρώπους θέλει σωθῆναι): Ael. Arist. 39, 11 (18, p. 411) (on the well of Asclepius) καὶ οὔτε ἐκεῖνος ἄγει σχολὴν ἄλλο τι πράττειν ἢ σῴζειν ἀνθρώπους καὶ τοῦτο μιμούμενον τὸν δεσπότην αἰεὶ πληροῖ τὴν τῶν δεομένων χρείαν. Note the different meanings of σῴζειν in Aristides and the N.T.

1 Tim. II 8 (προσεύχεσθαι ... ἐπαίροντας ... χεῖρας): Ael. Arist. 24, 50 (44, p. 840) οὐ τὰς χεῖρας ἄρας ἄνω σὺν αἰδοῖ καὶ δέει συγγνώμην αἰτήσει τῶν μέχρι τοῦδε ἡμαρτημένων τοὺς θεούς;

1 Tim. II 9 (μετὰ αἰδοῦς ... κοσμεῖν ἑαυτάς): Ael. Arist. 30, 18 (10, p. 120) αἰδῶ πολλὴν ἐπαμφιασαμένη ...

1 Tim. II 9-14: Ael. Arist. 2, 129 (45, p. 41) πολλὰ ... ὁ ἀνὴρ λεγέτω, γυνὴ δὲ οἷς ἂν ἀκούσῃ χαιρέτω. ἆρ' οὖν οὐκ εὔδηλον ὡς ὁ μὲν αὐτὸς εὑρηκὼς καὶ προειδὼς ἐρεῖ πολλά, ἣ δ' ἄρχεσθαι προσήκει, στέρξει τοῖς λεγομένοις; οὐ γὰρ δήπου τῆς γε γυναικὸς ἀκοῦσαι περιμένων, εἶτ' ἐρεῖ πρὸς τὴν γυναῖκα αὐτὸς τί δεῖ ποιεῖν.

1 Tim. II 13 ('Αδὰμ ... πρῶτος ἐπλάσθη): Ael. Arist. 42, 7 (6, p. 67) Προμηθεὺς τἀρχαῖα λέγεται συμπλάσαι τὸν ἄνθρωπον.

1 Tim. III 2.4.8.11 (σώφρων, σεμνός, Tit. II 2.4.5.7.9.12.15): Ael. Arist. 3, 12 (46, p. 159) (on Pericles) ἐκεῖνος τοίνυν λέγεται βιῶναι μὲν οὕτω σεμνῶς ὥστε μηδὲν τῶν προφητῶν καὶ τῶν ἱερέων τὸν ἐκείνου βίον διαφέρειν, οὕτω δὲ εἶναι σώφρων ὥστε καὶ βαδίζειν τεταγμένα καὶ τὴν ὀρθὴν ὁδὸν σῴζειν κατὰ τὴν παροιμίαν.

1 Tim. III 7 (οἱ ἔξωθεν): Ael. Arist. 1, 89 (13, p. 193) δείγματα τῆς πρὸς τοὺς ἔξωθεν φιλανθρωπίας.

1 Tim. IV 4 (πᾶν κτίσμα θεοῦ καλόν): Ael. Arist. 37, 2 (2, p. 13) πάντα μὲν οὖν κάλλιστα περὶ 'Αθηνᾶν τε καὶ ἐξ 'Αθηνᾶς.

1 Tim. IV 7 (γραώδεις μύθους): Ael. Arist. 2, 394 (45, p. 133) εἰ δὲ δεῖ καὶ μῦθον λέγειν, δέδοικα μὲν ἐγὼ μὴ καὶ ταῖς γραυσὶν ἡμᾶς ἐξούλης ὀφλεῖν ἐπισκώπτων φῇ τις ἀνὴρ κωμικός.

1 Tim. IV 10 (... θεῷ ζῶντι, ὅς ἐστιν σωτὴρ πάντων ἀνθρώπων, cf. II 4, Tit. II 11): Ael. Arist. 45, 20 (8, p. 90) Sarapis is called σωτῆρα πάντων ἀνθρώπων.

1 Tim. V 13 (λαλοῦσαι τὰ μὴ δέοντα): Ael. Arist. 2, 1 (45, p. 1) τὰ δέοντα ἐρεῖν. ibid. 387 (p. 130) and 391 (p. 132) λέγειν τὰ δέοντα.

1 Tim. V 17 (τιμῆς ἀξιούσθωσαν): Ael. Arist. 40, 10 (5, p. 57) ἠξιώκαμεν τιμῆς.

1 Tim. VI 4 (νοσέω used metaphorically, referring to strife and faction): Ael. Arist. 1, 255 (13, p. 272) ἐνόσησε (sc. ἡ πόλις) μὲν γὰρ τῇ τῶν ἀνθρώπων φύσει, ἰάθη δὲ τῇ ἑαυτῆς. Cf. also ibid. 261-2 (p. 273) where the scholiast explains νοσεῖν by στασιάζειν.

1 Tim. VI 11 (εὐσέβειαν, πίστιν): Ael. Arist. 1, 155 (13, p. 226) εὐσεβείας (sc. σύμβολον παρέσχοντο) μὲν διὰ τὴν πίστιν ἣν ἐν τοῖς θεοῖς εἶχον, sc. the Athenians in 480 B.C.

I Tim. VI 11 (ὑπομονὴν, πραϋπαθίαν): [Ael. Arist.] 25, 64 (43, p. 821) τὸ συμβεβηκὸς (sc. a calamity) ἐνεγκεῖν ὡς πραότατα.

I Tim. VI 12 (ἀγωνίζου τὸν ... ἀγῶνα, 2 Tim. IV 7): Ael. Arist. I, 115 (13, p. 206) ἀγῶνα διπλοῦν ἀγωνίζεται. I, 152 (13, p. 225) ... ἀγωνιζόμεθα οὐδὲν ἐλάττω κατὰ τοὺς λόγους ἀγῶνα μικροῦ δεῖν ἢ κατὰ τὰς πράξεις ἐκεῖνοι τότε. 25, 36 (43, p. 810) δεῖ δὴ κατὰ κράτος αὐτοῖς ἀνθίστασθαι καὶ παντὶ τῷ θυμῷ παρεσκευασμένους τὸν ἀγῶνα τοῦτον ἀγωνίζεσθαι. For the metaphor see *ad* I Cor. IX 25, and add 43, 5 (I, p. 2) δεῖ ... πειρᾶσθαι τοῦ ἀγωνίσματος.

2 Tim. I 3 (χάριν ἔχω τῷ θεῷ): Ael. Arist. 47, 74 (23, p. 464) τῷ τε θεῷ χάριν ἔχων.

2 Tim. I 9 (God acted πρὸ χρόνων αἰωνίων, Tit. I 2): Ael. Arist. 43, 10 (1, p. 3) Zeus ὢν χρόνου τε κρείττων.

2 Tim. I 10f. (διὰ τοῦ εὐαγγελίου εἰς ὃ ἐτέθην ἐγὼ κῆρυξ, cf. passim κηρύσσειν τὸ εὐαγγέλιον): Ael. Arist. 1, 299 (13, p. 285) καίτοι ἀφῖκτο μὲν κατ' ἀρχὰς εὐθὺς κῆρυξ παρὰ τῶν Θηβαίων ὡς ἐπ' εὐαγγελίοις ἐστεφανωμένος.

2 Tim. II 11b-12: Ael. Arist. 3, 559 (46, p. 364) εἰ δὲ εὐσχημόνως, καὶ τεταγμένως· εἰ δὲ τεταγμένως, καὶ κοσμίως. Actually this stylistic device (concatenation) in Aristides is a mixture of those found in 2 Tim. I 11b-12 and in 2 Peter I 5-7. See M. Dibelius, *Der Jakobusbrief* (1964²) 125-9.

2 Tim. II 15 (ὀρθοτομεῖν): Ael. Arist. 2, 324 (45, p. 106) δίκαιον ἂν ἴσως καὶ συμφέρον γένοιτο ἡμῖν πᾶσιν μέσον τεμεῖν (Behr: "to take a middle course").

2 Tim. II 22 (δίωκε δὲ δικαιοσύνην, πίστιν, ἀγάπην, εἰρήνην): Ael. Arist. 27, 44 (16, p. 399) νῦν χρὴ πάσας τὰς πόλεις ἀδελφὰς ἀλλήλαις ὑπολαμβάνειν, νῦν στάσεις μὲν καὶ ταραχὰς καὶ φιλονικίας καὶ τὸ μικρολογεῖσθαι περὶ τῶν ματαίων ἐκποδὼν ἀνελεῖν, νομίσαντας θηρίων εἶναι νοσήματα ταῦτα κἀκείνοις αὐτὰ παρεῖναι δεῖν, εἰρήνην δὲ ἀληθινὴν καὶ φιλίαν ἄδολον καὶ δικαιοσύνην καὶ τὴν διὰ πάντων εἰ οἷόν τε κοινωνίαν μέγιστον κερδῶν ὑπολαβεῖν. (N.B. φιλία does not occur in the N.T. except in φιλία τοῦ κόσμου in James IV 4).

2 Tim. II 25 (ἐν πραΰτητι παιδεύοντα τοὺς ἀντιδιατιθεμένους): Ael. Arist. 26, 96 (14, p. 364) ... τοὺς δὲ βαρβάρους πρὸς τὴν ἑκάστοις αὐτῶν οὖσαν φύσιν παιδεύοντες πραότερόν τε καὶ σφοδρότερον.

2 Tim. III 11 (διωγμοὺς ὑπήνεγκα, καὶ ἐκ πάντων με ἐρρύσατο ὁ κύριος): Ael. Arist. 50, 9 (26, p. 504) ἡ λοιμώδης ἐκείνη συνέβη νόσος, ἧς ὅ τε Σωτὴρ καὶ ἡ δέσποινα Ἀθηνᾶ περιφανῶς ἐρρύσαντό με.

2 Tim. III 14 (μένε ἐν οἷς ἔμαθες): Ael. Arist. 2, 119 (45, p. 38) οἱ τῇ δυνάμει πρωτεύσαντες ἐντίμους τὰς τέχνας ἐποίησαν, οὐ μείναντες ἐφ' ὧν παρέλαβον. (For παραλαμβάνω see *ad* 1 Cor. XI 23).

TITUS

Tit. I 7f. (τὸν ἐπίσκοπον ... μὴ αὐθάδη ... σώφρονα ...): Ael. Arist. 8, 14 (32, p. 606) σωφρονίσαι τὴν αὐθάδειαν αὐτῶν.

Tit. I 8 (σώφρονα, δίκαιον, ὅσιον, ἐγκρατῆ; compare in general the terminology of the Pastoral Epistles): [Ael. Arist.] 35, 15 (9, p. 103) ... ὅνπερ χρὴ τρόπον τὸν εὐσέβειαν μὲν καὶ δικαιοσύνην, ἔτι δὲ σωφροσύνην καὶ ἐγκράτειαν καὶ φρόνησιν καὶ τὴν ἄλλην κοσμοῦντα ἀρετήν. Cf. *ad* Tit. II 12.

Tit. I 13 (metaphorical use of ὑγιαίνειν applied to men, cf. II 2): Ael. Arist. 2, 29 (45, p. 10) ἀλλ' οὔτε τοῦτο ὑγιαίνοντος, οἶμαι, οὔτ' ἐκεῖνο ἀποδεικνύντος.

Tit. II 12 (σωφρόνως καὶ δικαίως): Ael. Arist. 32, 18 (12, p. 140) ἡ σωφροσύνη καὶ τὸ δίκαιον.

Tit. III 3 (δουλεύοντες ἐπιθυμίαις καὶ ἡδοναῖς): Ael. Arist. 2, 195 (45, p. 59) δουλεύουσι ταῖς ἐπιθυμίαις. 6, 42 (30, p. 585) οὐδεὶς γὰρ ἀνθρώπων ἐκ προρρήσεως ἅπαντα κατεργάζεται, οὐδ' οἱ πόλεμοι δουλεύουσι ταῖς ἐπιθυμίαις. Cf. 35, 27 (9, p. 107-8) ὅσαι ἡδοναὶ ἄρχουσιν ἀνθρώπων οὐδεμιᾶς ἴσμεν ἡττημένον τὸν βασιλεά. ... ἀκολαστότατοι περὶ τὰς ἡδονὰς καὶ τὰς ἐπιθυμίας ὄντες ἐφάνησαν. For ἡττᾶσθαι in this connection see 2 Peter II 19b.

Tit. III 4 (ἡ φιλανθρωπία ἐπεφάνη τοῦ σωτῆρος ἡμῶν θεοῦ): Ael. Arist. 45, 26 (8, p. 93) φιλανθρωπότατος γὰρ θεῶν, sc. Σάραπις. 37, 17 (2, p. 20) φιλανθρωποτάτη δὲ ἡ αὐτὴ (sc. Ἀθηνᾶ) ... τὴν δὲ φιλανθρωπίαν οἱ περὶ Ὀρέστην λόγοι μαρτύρονται. 39, 5 (18, p. 409) θεῶν... ὁ φιλανθρωπότατος, sc. Ἀσκληπιός. ibid. 11 (p. 411). 41, 10 (4, p. 51) φιλάνθρωπος, sc. Διόνυσος. 42, 12 (6, p. 68) τῆς σῆς φιλανθρωπίας (sc. of Asclepius). 46, 9 (3, p. 32) πότερος αὐτῶν (sc. of the gods) τὴν ἀρχὴν φιλανθρωποτέραν ἐποιήσατο τὴν αὑτοῦ. 38, 15 (7, p. 76) on the Asclepiads, ἡ τούτων ... φιλανθρωπία ... ἔσωσε καὶ σῴζει (cf. σωτῆρος in Tit. III 4 and ἔσωσεν in v. 5). ibid. 24 (p. 80). φιλανθρωπία of common people is also mentioned by Aristides (as in Acts XXVII 3 and XXVIII 2), but esp. of rulers, e.g. 35, 1 (9, p. 98) περὶ τοῦ θείου καὶ φιλανθρώπου βασιλέως. 26, 98 (14, p. 365) τὴν ὁμοίαν εἰς ἅπαντας ὑμῶν (sc. of the Romans) φιλανθρωπίαν. Cf. 1, 155 (13, p. 226) φιλανθρωπίας δὲ (sc. σύμβολον παρέσχοντο) ὅτι ταῦτα ὑπὲρ τῆς τῶν ἄλλων σωτηρίας ὑπέμενον, sc. the Athenians. See further 26, 57 (14, p. 345) and 66 (p. 349).

Hebr. I 4 (τοσούτῳ κρείττων γενόμενος τῶν ἀγγέλων): Ael. Arist. 37, 7 (2, p. 15) the goddess Athena ἀγγέλου ... ἐστι μείζων.

Hebr. I 6 (εἰσαγάγῃ τὸν πρωτότοκον εἰς τὴν οἰκουμένην): Ael. Arist. 43, 15 (1, p. 6) Zeus εἶτα τοὺς ἄνδρας εἰσῆγεν, sc. into the world.

Hebr. I 10 (σὺ κατ' ἀρχὰς ... τὴν γῆν ἐθεμελίωσας = Ps. CII 25): Ael. Arist. 43, 11 (1, p. 4) Zeus ἄρχεται ἐκ θεμελίων καὶ ποιεῖ γῆν.

Hebr. II 3 (ἀρχὴν λαβοῦσα): Ael. Arist. 1, 25 (13, p. 163) ὥσπερ τὸ ἐκ τῶν πηγῶν ὕδωρ ἐκ τῶν κόλπων τῆς γῆς ἀνῆλθε τὸ γένος, αὐτὸ ἐξ αὑτοῦ λαβὸν τὴν ἀρχήν.

Hebr. II 10 (δι' ὃν τὰ πάντα καὶ δι' οὗ τὰ πάντα): Ael. Arist. 45, 14 (8, p. 87) (said to Sarapis) πάντα γὰρ πανταχοῦ διὰ σοῦ τε καὶ διὰ σὲ ἡμῖν γίγνεται. Cf. 43, 23 (1, p. 9) διὰ τοῦτον (sc. Δία) ἅπαντα γίγνεται ... δι' αὐτὸν ἅπαντα γίγνεταί τε καὶ γέγονε. In John I 3, Rom. XI 36, 1 Cor. VIII 6, Col. I 16 we find only δι' αὐτοῦ; it is only in Hebr. that both the accusative and the genitive are found.

Hebr. III 4 (ὁ δὲ πάντα κατασκευάσας θεός): Ael. Arist. 43, 15 (1, p. 6) Zeus κατεσκευάσατο τὸν κόσμον. Cf. 37, 14 (2, p. 18).

Hebr. III 5 (Moses as θεράπων of God): Ael. Arist. 39, 5 (18, p. 409) ἡμῖν ... τοῖς τούτου (sc. of Asclepius) θεράπουσιν.

Hebr. III 13 (καθ' ἑκάστην ἡμέραν): Ael. Arist. 12, 49 (34, p. 661) πολλοὶ καθ' ἡμέραν ἑκάστην ἐγίγνοντο. The expression καθ' ἡμέραν ἑκάστην is actually pleonastic; hence some mss. omit καθ', others omit ἑκάστην. Cf. 26, 87 (14, p. 359).

Hebr. IV 13 (πάντα δὲ γυμνὰ ... τοῖς ὀφθαλμοῖς αὐτοῦ): Ael. Arist. 43, 27 (1, p. 10) οὐ νὺξ ἔμπροσθεν ἵσταται, οὐχ ὕπνος τῶν τούτου (sc. Διός) μεγάλων τε καὶ μόνων ἑωρακότων τἀληθὲς ὀφθαλμῶν.

Hebr. IV 16 (God's εὔκαιρος βοήθεια): Ael. Arist. 43, 30 (1, p. 11) Zeus is ἐν ... πᾶσιν καιροῖς βοηθῶν.

Hebr. V 6 (κατὰ τὴν τάξιν Μελχισέδεκ, V 10, VI 20, VII 11, 17): Ael. Arist. 1, 94 (13, p. 196) ἐν Βαβυλῶνος τάξει καὶ τῶν ἐν Ἰνδοῖς Ἕλληνες Σάρδεις ἐθαύμαζον. 28, 97 (49, p. 523) σὺ δ' ἡμῖν οὐδὲ τοσοῦτον μετέδωκας ἀναπνεῦσαι, καὶ ταῦτα ὢν οὐδείς, ἀλλ' ἀγαπᾶν σοι προσῆκον, εἰ καὶ ἐν οἰκέτου τάξει παρῆσθα τοῖς γιγνομένοις.

Hebr. V 9 (Jesus as αἴτιος σωτηρίας αἰωνίου): Ael. Arist. 43, 23 (1, p. 9) Ζεὺς αἴτιος (sc. πάντων τῶν ὄντων).

Hebr. V 12.14 (τροφή = spiritual food): Ael. Arist. 1, 2 (13, p. 150) ... περὶ ἧς εἶχον ἐν νῷ τροφῆς εἰπεῖν, τῆς ὡς ἀληθῶς καθαρᾶς καὶ διαφερόντως ἀνθρώπου, τῆς ἐν μαθήμασι καὶ λόγοις.

Hebr. VI 17 (τὸ ἀμετάθετον τῆς βουλῆς αὐτοῦ, sc. θεοῦ): Ael. Arist. 43, 22 (1, p. 8) οὐ θέμις αὐτῷ (sc. Διί) ... ἑτέραν γνώμην ἔχειν. ibid. 25 (p. 9) Διὸς νημερτέα βουλήν (= *Hymn. in Ap.* 132).

Hebr. VI 18 (οἱ καταφυγόντες, sc. to God): Ael. Arist. 2, 69 (45, p. 22) καταφυγεῖν ἐπὶ τοὺς θεούς. 47, 17 (23, p. 449) προσευχομένου δέ μου καὶ ἀνακαλοῦντος τὸν θεὸν ὁ Ζήνων 'οὐδέν', ἔφη, 'προσηνέστερον', λέγων δὴ καὶ αὐτὸς τὸν θεόν, καταφυγήν τε καὶ τοιαῦτα ὠνόμαζεν.

Hebr. VI 18-19 (... καταφυγόντες ... ἄγκυραν ... ἀσφαλῆ ... τὸ ἐσώτερον τοῦ καταπετάσματος ... ἀρχιερεύς): Ael. Arist. 3, 252 (46, p. 258) οἱ δ' ἐπείθοντο, καὶ καταλιπόντες ἱερὰ καὶ τάφους καὶ γῆν εἰς ἕνα ἑώρων Θεμιστοκλέα, παίδων καὶ γονέων καὶ τῶν τῆς φύσεως ἀναγκαίων ἐκεῖνον προκρίναντες, καὶ ὥσπερ τῆς ἱερᾶς ἀγκύρας τῆς ἐκείνου φωνῆς ἐχόμενοι. (*scholion ad loc.*: ἀπὸ παροιμίας εἴρηται ἡ ἱερὰ ἄγκυρα· σημαίνει δὲ τὴν καταφυγὴν τὴν γιγνομένην εἰς τὰ ἱερά, ἥτις ἦν ἀσφάλεια καὶ ἀσυλία τοῖς εἰς αὐτὰ καταφεύγουσιν.) For the image of the anchor see also 1, 54 (13, p. 176) καὶ πάντες ἐπὶ δυοῖν ὁρμεῖν ἔδοξαν οἱ Ἕλληνες (and all the Greeks thought that they were secured by two anchors, viz. their place of origin and the city of Athens). Cf. the scholion: παροιμία τὸ ἐπὶ δυοῖν ὁρμεῖν ἐπὶ τῶν ἀσφαλῶς πρός τι χωρούντων. Cf. also 23, 17 (42, p. 773) Pergamon is the haven where πᾶσιν ἐξ Ἀσκληπιοῦ τὰ ἐπίγυια τῆς σωτηρίας ἤρτηται.

Hebr. VI 20 (Jesus as πρόδρομος): Ael. Arist. 37, 29 (2, p. 27) Athena as πρόδρομος.

Hebr. VII 2.4.6.8.9 (δεκάτη, δεκατοῦν): Ael. Arist. 45, 28 (8, p. 94) ἐμπόρων ... δεκάτας ἀναγόντων (sc. τῷ Σαράπιδι).

Hebr. VII 9 (ὡς ἔπος εἰπεῖν): this idiomatic expression occurs only here in the N.T., but is very frequent in Greek literature, especially in the orators. In Ael. Arist. it occurs at least about thirty times, sometimes in the variant form ὡς εἰπεῖν. Some references may suffice: for ὡς ἔπος εἰπεῖν 1, 50 (13, p. 173); 2, 40 (45, p. 12), ibid. 148 (p. 47) and 197 (p. 60); 27, 15 (16, p. 388); 36, 54 (48, p. 461); 45, 4 (8, p. 83); 39, 10 (18, p. 411); etc.; for ὡς εἰπεῖν 1, 242 (13, p. 267); 1, 375 (13, p. 312); 27, 8 (16, p. 386); 31, 3 (11, p. 127); 38, 23 (7, p. 79); 40, 5 (5, p. 54); 43, 4 (1, p. 2).

Hebr. VII 11 (νομοθετεῖν, νομοθέτης, νομοθεσία, always with God as subject; VIII 6, James IV 12; cf. Rom. IX 4): Ael. Arist. 43, 20 (1, p. 8) ταῦτα δὲ ἐνομοθέτει Ζεύς.

Hebr. VIII 1 (κεφάλαιον δὲ ἐπὶ τοῖς λεγομένοις ...): Ael. Arist. 1, 349 (13, p. 304) ἵνα δ' εἴπω κεφάλαιον ... (*scholion ad loc.* κεφάλαιον· καθολικὸν καὶ σύντομον λόγον). 11, 70 (33, p. 641) κεφάλαιον δ' εἰπὼν καὶ δὴ πέπαυμαι. 15, 40 (37, p. 709) ὡς δ' εἰπεῖν κεφάλαιον,... 28, 70 (49, p. 514) καὶ τὸ μὲν κεφάλαιον ὅπερ λέγω τῆς σπουδῆς τοῦτ' ἔστιν. 37, 2 (2, p. 13) κεφάλαιον μὲν εἰπεῖν ὅτι ... 37, 27 (2, p. 27) ὡς δ' εἰπεῖν ἐν κεφαλαίῳ, ...

Hebr. VIII 8 (μεμφόμενος ... λέγει, sc. God): Ael. Arist. 43, 4 (1, p. 2) μέμψιν ἐκ θεῶν.

Hebr. VIII 12 (ἵλεως ἔσομαι κτλ. = Jer. XXXI 34): Ael. Arist. 46, 4 (3, p. 30) οἷς ἂν ἵλεως ὢν τυγχάνῃ, sc. ὁ θεός.

Hebr. X 31: Ael. Arist. 45, 26 (8, p. 93) φοβερώτατος ὁ αὐτός, sc. Sarapis.

Hebr. XI 7 (κληρονόμος in a spiritual sense): Ael. Arist. 15, 29 (37, p. 705) τῆς ἐκείνου πονηρίας καὶ ἀπιστίας κληρονόμους εἶναι προσῆκον οὐδαμῶς ὑμῖν ἐστιν.

Hebr. XI 8 (ὑπακούειν, sc. θεῷ): Ael. Arist. 52, 1 (28, p. 551) ὁ θεὸς ... ἔχων ὑπακούοντας, εἴ τις καὶ ἄλλος ἀνθρώπων ὑπήκουσεν θεῷ.

Hebr. XI 10 (only here in the N.T. God is called δημιουργός): in Ael. Arist. Zeus is called δημιουργός in 43, 14.15.23 (1, pp. 5.6.9) and in 37, 2 (2, p. 13).

Hebr. XI 27 (καρτερεῖν only here in the N.T.): Ael. Arist. 48, 42 (24, p. 476) Athena tells Aristides in a vision that he should καρτερεῖν.

Hebr. XI 32 (καὶ τί ἔτι λέγω; ἐπιλείψει με γὰρ διηγούμενον ὁ χρόνος περὶ κτλ.): Ael. Arist. 1, 317 (13, p. 292) ἔχων δὲ πολλὰ καὶ τῶν ὕστερον εἰπεῖν καὶ μάχας ἀτόπους καὶ τολμήματα θαυμαστὰ καὶ καρτερίας ὑπερφυεῖς, οὐκέθ' ὁρῶ τὸν καιρὸν ἀρκοῦντα. 17, 7 (15, p. 373) ... πολλῆς τινος ἔργον σχολῆς διηγήσασθαι. ἀλλὰ τί δεῖ περὶ ταῦτα τρίβεσθαι; 32, 4 (12, p. 135) ἀθρόα γὰρ πάντα ἐπέρχεται, ἃ καθ' ἕκαστον μὲν εἰπεῖν ἀδύνατον, ἀρχὴν δὲ οὐδὲ πειρᾶσθαι καιρὸν ἔχειν μοι δοκεῖ. 35, 2 (9, p. 98) ἃ τοῖς προοιμιαζομένοις λέγειν ἔθος ἐστὶν καὶ προφασίζεσθαι, τοῖς μὲν τὸ μέγεθος τῶν πεπραγμένων, τοῖς δὲ τὸν χρόνον ὀλίγον ὄντα τῶν λόγων. Cf. further 35, 3 (9, p. 99) and 1, 92 (13, p. 195).

Hebr. XII 2 (τὸν τῆς πίστεως ἀρχηγὸν καὶ τελειωτήν): Ael. Arist. 43, 31 (1, p. 11) τὸν ἁπάντων κρατοῦντα ἀρχηγέτην καὶ τέλειον μόνον αὐτὸν ὄντα τῶν πάντων, sc. Zeus.

Hebr. XIII 6 (κύριος ἐμοὶ βοηθός = Ps. CXVIII 7): Ael. Arist. 43, 30 (1, p. 11) Zeus as βοηθῶν. 45, 14 (8, p. 87) σὲ γὰρ δὴ πᾶς τις ἐν παντὶ καιρῷ βοηθὸν καλεῖ, Σάραπι.

Hebr. XIII 12 (ἔξω τῆς πύλης ἔπαθεν, sc. Jesus): [Ael. Arist.] 25, 28 (43, p. 807) καὶ πρότερον μέν, ὦ Ζεῦ, τὰς φονικὰς δίκας ἔξω πυλῶν ἐδικάζετε, ὡς οὐδὲ καταψηφίσασθαι θάνατον ἐντὸς τείχους εὐσεβῶς ἔχον ὑμῖν.

Hebr. XIII 14 (the world as πόλις): Ael. Arist. 43, 15 (1, p. 6) ὥσπερ πόλιν ποιῶν αὐτήν (sc. τὴν γῆν).

Hebr. XIII 20 (τὸν ποιμένα τῶν προβάτων ..., τὸν κύριον ἡμῶν 'Ιησοῦν, 1 Ptr. II 25; cf. John X 11 and 14); Ael. Arist. 26, 18 (14, p. 330) it is said of the Persian kings that they are οὐδὲ τημελοῦντες ὥσπερ νομεῖς.

Hebr. XIII 22 (διὰ βραχέων ἐπέστειλα ὑμῖν, i.e. in chapters I-XIII!): Ael. Arist. 1, 67 (13, p. 183) τοῦτο δὴ βούλομαι διὰ βραχέων ἐπανελθὼν ἐξετάσαι, i.e. in paragraphs 67-74. Cf. 3, 214 (46, p. 240) ... δεῖξαι διὰ βραχέων ἐν ποίοις τισὶ πράγμασι ποῖός τις ἦν ὁ Θεμιστοκλῆς. 36, 1 (48, p. 437) ... σοι διὰ βραχέων καὶ ἐπιπολῆς ἀπεκρινάμην.

JAMES

Jas. I 3 (1 Ptr. I 7): [Ael. Arist.] 25, 36 (43, p. 811) ὅλως δὲ ὥσπερ τὸν χρυσὸν ἡ βάσανος δείκνυσιν, οὕτω τοὺς ἄνδρας τοὺς ἀγαθοὺς κρίνουσιν αἱ συμφοραί.

Jas. I 4 (τέλειοι καὶ ὁλόκληροι): [Ael. Arist.], *Ars Rhet.* I 1 (Schmid) ὁλόκληρος καὶ τελείως ἔχων, sc. ὁ λόγος.

Jas. I 5 (τοῦ διδόντος θεοῦ πᾶσιν ἁπλῶς): Ael. Arist. 3, 497 (46, p. 345) ... ἀφειδῶς καὶ ἁπλῶς δόντες αὑτοὺς ὑπὲρ τοῦ κοινῇ βελτίστου.

Jas. I 17a: Ael. Arist. 1, 192 (13, p. 242) τούς τε γὰρ θεοὺς ὡς αἰτίους δήπου τῶν ἀγαθῶν ἀμειβόμεθα. 45, 15 (8, p. 88) ὅσων δὲ καὶ οἵων ἀγαθῶν αἴτιος ἀνθρώποις δείκνυται, sc. Sarapis. 46, 36 (3, p. 44) κακὰ γὰρ οὔτε ἔστιν ἐν θεοῖς, ἀλλ' οὐδ' ἂν δύναιτο γενέσθαι ποτέ - ... κακὰ γὰρ ἐκ κακῶν, ἀγαθὰ δὲ ἔργα τὰ θεῶν.

Jas. I 17b: Ael. Arist. 43, 22 (1, p. 8) οὐ γὰρ θέμις αὐτῷ (sc. Διί) μεταστραφῆναι οὐδὲ ἑτέραν γνώμην ἔχειν οὔτε ὑπὸ λήθης οὔτε ὑπὸ μετανοίας ἧς ἔσχεν ἐξ ἀρχῆς. 1, 47 (13, p. 172) καὶ μεταβολὴ τοῦ χωρίου τούτου μόνου (sc. the Areopagus) ἤδη σχεδὸν οὐχ ἥψατο, οἷα δὴ τὰ ἀνθρώπινα, ἀλλ' ὥσπερ ἀγωνιστήριον τοῖς θεοῖς ἀνεῖται.

Jas. II 1-9: Ael. Arist. 1, 390 (13, p. 316) καὶ μὴν ἐκεῖνό γε ἡ πόλις πρώτη κατέδειξεν, μὴ τίθεσθαι πλούτῳ μηδὲ θαυμάζειν. οὔτε γὰρ τοὺς ὑπερέχοντας ταῖς οὐσίαις οὐδεπώποτε ἐπῆρεν, ἀλλ' ὅσον μὴ ἀδικεῖσθαι διὰ τοῦτο, τοσοῦτον αὐτοῖς ἠξίου παρ' αὐτῆς ὀφείλεσθαι, οὔτε τοῖς ἀρέτῃ μὲν ὑπερφέρουσι, χρήμασι δ' ἡττημένοις, οὐδαμοῦ πώποτ' ἔλαττον ἔνειμεν, αἰσχρὸν οἶμαι νομίζουσα τῶν μὲν οἰκετῶν οὐ τοὺς εὐπορωτάτους, ἀλλὰ τοὺς πιστοτάτους βελτίστους νομίζειν, τῶν δ' ἐλευθέρων φασκόντων εἶναι τὴν ἀξίαν ὡρίσθαι χρήμασιν, ἀλλὰ μὴ ὁποῖός τις ἂν αὐτὸς ἕκαστος ᾖ, τοιοῦτον καὶ νομίζεσθαι.

Jas. II 15 (λειπόμενοι τῆς ἐφημέρου τροφῆς): Ael. Arist. 28, 139 (49, p. 537) τῆς ἐφημέρου τροφῆς ἀπορῶν.

Jas. III 2 (εἴ τις ἐν λόγῳ οὐ πταίει, οὗτος τέλειος ἀνήρ): Ael. Arist. 34, 62 (50, p. 570) κἂν μὲν ῥήματι πταίσῃ τις, ἀμαθὴς εὐθέως.

Jas. III 2f. (χαλιναγωγεῖν in relation to words; cf. I 26): Ael. Arist. 50, 45 (26, p. 516) οὐκ ἀφανὴς Ἕλλησιν Ἀριστείδης ἀνέθηκεν | μύθων ἀενάων κύδιμος ἡνίοχος (an epigram).

Jas. IV 7 (ὑποτάγητε οὖν τῷ θεῷ): Ael. Arist. 47, 4 (23, p. 446) ἐγνώκειν παρέχειν (= to submit myself) ... τῷ θεῷ.

Jas. IV 12 (εἷς ἐστιν νομοθέτης, sc. God): Ael. Arist. 1, 382 (13, p. 314) αὐτοῖς ὁ θεὸς συνέταξε τὸ κατ' ἀρχὰς τοὺς νόμους. ... οὐχ ἧττον ἂν εἴη τῆς πόλεως ὁ θεὸς νομοθέτης ἢ ἐκείνων.

Jas. IV 13 (εἰς τήνδε τὴν πόλιν): Ael. Arist. 3, 622 (46, p. 384) εἰς τήνδε τὴν ἡμέραν. For τήνδε instead of τὴν δεῖνα or τὴν καὶ τὴν see Bauer's *Wörterbuch* s.v. ὅδε 3.

Jas. IV 14 (ἀτμὶς γάρ ἐστε πρὸς ὀλίγον φαινομένη, ἔπειτα καὶ ἀφανιζομένη): Ael. Arist. 31, 17 (11, p. 131) βίος δὲ πᾶς ἀνθρώπου βραχὺς καὶ οὐ πολλοῦ τινος ἄξιος εἰς ἀριθμοῦ λόγον.

Jas. V 15 (σώσει τὸν κάμνοντα = will heal the sick): Ael. Arist. 2, 258 (45, p. 80) ἕως ἂν ἰατρικὴ σῴζῃ τοὺς κάμνοντας. Cf. 33, 9 (51, p. 573).

1 PETER

1 Ptr. I 7 (εἰς ἔπαινον καὶ δόξαν καὶ τιμήν): [Ael. Arist.] 35, 38 (9, p. 112) ἀνθ' ὧν οὐκ ἂν γένοιτο ἀξία σοι χάρις παρ' ἡμῶν οὔτ' ἐν ἐπαίνοις οὔτ' ἐν ἄλλῃ οὐδεμιᾷ τιμῇ.

1 Ptr. I 8 (χαρᾷ ἀνεκλαλήτῳ): Ael. Arist. 48, 33 (24, p. 474) δάκρυα σὺν χαρᾷ ... τίς ἀνθρώπων ταῦτά γ' ἐνδείξασθαι λόγῳ δυνατός;

1 Ptr. II 11 (ἀπέχεσθαι τῶν σαρκικῶν ἐπιθυμιῶν): [Ael. Arist.] 35, 27 (9, p. 107-8) τοσοῦτον γὰρ ἀπέσχεν αὐτῶν (sc. ἡδονῶν) εὐθὺς ἐξ ἀρχῆς ὥστε, εἴ τίς ἐστιν ἐγκράτεια κατ' ἀνθρώπους ὑμνουμένη, ταύτην περὶ τούτου μόνου λεγομένην πιστὴν εἶναι δοκεῖν. τίς μὲν γὰρ οὕτω γαστρὸς ἐγκρατής, τίς δὲ ἀφροδισίων, τίς δὲ τῶν ἄλλων ἡδονῶν; For ἐγκράτεια, ἐγκρατής see Acts XXIV 25, 1 Cor. VII 9, Gal. V 23, Tit. I 8, 2 Ptr. I 6.

1 Ptr. II 19 (anti-parallel): Ael. Arist. 12, 35 (34, p. 656) ὅλως μὲν γὰρ οὐκ ἔστι φέρειν ἀδικούμενον.

1 Ptr. II 25 (God as ἐπίσκοπος τῶν ψυχῶν): Ael. Arist. 43, 29 (1, p. 11) οὗτος (sc. Ζεύς) ... ἔφορος.

1 Ptr. III 1-2: [Ael. Arist.] 35, 26 (9, p. 107) ..., οὐκ ἐκστὰς ἑαυτοῦ οὐδὲ ζηλώσας τὴν ἀκολασίαν, ἀλλὰ τὸν σώφρονα βίον ἑλόμενος, τὴν μὲν ὕβριν καὶ παρανομίαν μισήσας, παράδειγμα δὲ σωφροσύνης ἑαυτὸν παρασχών, ὥστε τοὺς τέως ἀσελγεῖς καὶ ὑβριστὰς μεταθέσθαι τὸν τρόπον ὁρῶντας αὐτοῦ τὴν σωφροσύνην, καὶ τῆς τε πρὸς τὰ χρήματα ἐπιθυμίας παύσασθαι καὶ πρὸς τὸ σωφρονέστερον διαθεῖναι.

1 Ptr. III 3 (ἐνδύσεως ἱματίων κόσμος): Ael. Arist. 37, 11 (2, p. 16) ἐσθῆτα, ... κόσμον τῷ σώματι.

1 Ptr. III 3-4 (hidden spiritual beauty): Ael. Arist. 23, 76 (42, p. 794) οὗτος (sc. the inner harmony) ὁ τῶν πόλεων κόσμος ἀληθινός, τοῦτο μέγιστον φυλακτήριον, τοῦτο σχῆμα κάλλιστον.

1 Ptr. III 10 (ἰδεῖν ἡμέρας ἀγαθάς = Ps. XXXIV 13): Ael. Arist. 8, 1 (32, p. 601) ἣν μὲν ἐκ πολλοῦ πάντες ἡμέραν ἰδεῖν ἐποθοῦμεν, ἥδ' ἐστίν.

1 Ptr. III 18 (ἵνα ἡμᾶς προσαγάγῃ τῷ θεῷ, cf. Rom. V 2, Eph. II 18, III 12): Ael. Arist. 50, 86 (26, p. 527) προσῆγεν ἡμᾶς τῷ ἡγεμόνι.

2 PETER

2 Ptr. I 4 (θείας κοινωνοὶ φύσεως): Ael. Arist. 2, 410 (45, p. 139) τῆς οὖν θείας φύσεως εἰκότως μετέχουσι μόνοι, sc. οἱ λόγοι. 50, 70 (26, p. 522) καὶ περὶ τῆς αὐτοῦ (sc. τοῦ θεοῦ) φύσεως ὁποῖ' ἄττα ἔδειξεν (sc. ὁ θεός) κτλ. Cf. also 37, 9 (2, p. 16) τὸ ἔργον αὐτῆς ὑπὲρ θεῶν τε καὶ τῆς θείας φύσεως ἁπάσης, and 43, 16 (1, p. 7) ἅτε τοῦ λόγου κεκοινωνηκὸς καὶ οὐ παντάπασιν ἀπηλλαγμένον τῆς θείας μοίρας.

2 Ptr. I 16 (τὴν τοῦ κυρίου ἡμῶν ... δύναμιν καὶ παρουσίαν): Ael. Arist. 48, 30 (24, p. 473) παρουσίαν καὶ δυνάμεις τινὰς τοῦ θεοῦ.

2 Ptr. I 17 (παρὰ θεοῦ πατρὸς τιμήν, cf. John V 44 and XII 26): Ael. Arist. 1, 38 (13, p. 168) τιμὴν παρὰ τῶν θεῶν. ibid. 49 (p. 172) τῆς ἐκ θεῶν τιμῆς. ibid. 338 (p. 301) ἡ ἐκ τῶν θεῶν τιμή ... τῆς μὲν παρὰ τῶν θεῶν τιμῆς. 50, 13 (26, p. 505) τὰς παρὰ τοῦ θεοῦ τιμάς. ibid. 51 (p. 518) τῆς ... τιμῆς παρὰ τοῦ θεοῦ. Cf. 41, 3 (4, p. 48) αὐτὸν ὁ Ζεὺς ἐτίμησε.

2 Ptr. II 5 (cf. Mt. XXIV 37ff., Lk. XII 26ff.): Ael. Arist. 24, 39 (44, p. 836) ἆρ' ἄλλο τι λείπεσθαι ἢ τοσούτων ἀνδρῶν καὶ γυναικῶν ἕνα καὶ μίαν λειφθῆναι, καθάπερ τοὺς ἐκ τοῦ κατακλυσμοῦ λέγουσιν;

2 Ptr. II 13 (ἡδονὴν ἡγούμενοι τὴν ἐν ἡμέρᾳ τρυφήν): [Ael. Arist.] 35, 30 (9, p. 109) ... οὐδὲ ἐν ἡδυπαθείᾳ καὶ τρυφῇ ὄντας διάγειν.

1 JOHN

1 John I 5 (ὁ θεὸς φῶς ἐστι): Ael. Arist. 28, 114 (49, p. 528) τὸ τοῦ θεοῦ φῶς.

1 John II 7: Ael. Arist. 29, 9 (40, p. 754) οὐδὲν καινὸν λέγω, ἀλλὰ πάλαι ταῦτα ἀνωμολόγηται κἀν τοῖς νόμοις κἀν τοῖς ἔθεσι τοῖς κοινοῖς.

1 John II 25 (ἡ ἐπαγγελία ἣν αὐτὸς ἐπηγγείλατο): Ael. Arist. 7, 18 (31, p. 596) τὰς σεμνὰς ἐκείνας ἐπαγγελίας ἐπαγγελλόμενοι.

1 John II 28 (ἵνα ... μὴ αἰσχυνθῶμεν): Ael. Arist. 43, 1 (1, p. 1) ὡς μὴ ... καταγέλαστοι γενώμεθα.

1 John III 8 (ἵνα λύσῃ τὰ ἔργα τοῦ διαβόλου): Ael. Arist. 41, 7 (4, p. 49) καὶ οὐδὲν ἄρα οὕτως βεβαίως δεδήσεται, οὐ νόσῳ, οὐκ ὀργῇ, οὐ τύχῃ οὐδεμιᾷ, ὃ μὴ οἷόν τ' ἔσται λῦσαι τῷ Διονύσῳ.

[2 John 9 (*varia lectio* ὁ παραβαίνων, substantivized and without object): Ael. Arist. 1, 194 (13, p. 243) ἀμείνων μὲν ὁ ποιῶν οἶμαι τὰ δίκαια ἀναγκαίως τοῦ παραβαίνοντος ἑκόντος.]

JUDE

Jude 3 (τῆς κοινῆς ἡμῶν σωτηρίας): Ael. Arist. 2, 323 (45, p. 106) τῆς κοινῆς τῶν Ἑλλήνων σωτηρίας. 3, 176 (46, p. 224) ἐπιόντων τῶν βαρβάρων τοῖς Ἕλλησιν οὐδὲν πρότερον τῆς κοινῆς σωτηρίας ἐποιήσατο. Cf. ibid. 240 (p. 252). 24, 26 (44, p. 832) . . . τὴν κοινὴν τῆς πόλεως σωτηρίαν προτέραν τῶν ἰδίων ἐγκλημάτων ποιησάμενος. 38, 18 (7, p. 77) Ἀσκληπιάδαι . . . κοινὴ πᾶσιν ἀσφάλεια καὶ σωτηρία γεγόνασιν.

Jude 4 (τὸν μόνον δεσπότην καὶ κύριον ἡμῶν): Ael. Arist. 1, 117 (13, p. 207) Xerxes said πάντων δ' εἶναι τούτων κύριος . . . εἰ . . . τὸν κοινὸν δεσπότην γνοῖεν.

Jude 5 (ὑπομνῆσαι δὲ ὑμᾶς βούλομαι): Ael. Arist. 12, 2 (34, p. 642) ἀναμνῆσαι δ' ὑμᾶς πρῶτον βούλομαι . . .

Jude 6 (ἀρχή in the local sense of realm, sc. of the angels): Ael. Arist. 1, 19 (13, p. 161) Athens is called τὴν τοῦ Διὸς ἀρχήν.

Jude 6 (οἰκητήριον used of (part of) heaven): Ael. Arist. 43, 14 (1, p. 5) heaven is called κάλλιστόν τε καὶ λαμπρότατον οἰκητηρίων καὶ ἁγνότατον.

Jude 13 (ὁ ζόφος τοῦ σκότους): Ael. Arist. 24, 44 (44, p. 838) περὶ δὲ αὐτὴν ὥσπερ δίκτυον ἐν κύκλῳ ζόφος καὶ σκότος.

APOCALYPSE

Apoc. I 1 (σημαίνειν with God as subject): Ael. Arist. 2, 127 (45, p. 40) ... τῷ πιστεῦσαι δικαιότερον ἢ ᾧ θεοὺς μὲν εὑρεῖν ἕκαστα τίθεμεν καὶ νῦν ἔτι σημαίνειν; ... εἰς θεοὺς ἀνενεγκεῖν τὴν εὕρεσιν, εἴπερ εὑρόντος μέν ἐστι σημῆναι, εὑρίσκει δὲ ὁ κρείττων ἀεί. 47, 55 (23, p. 459) ἐδεόμην δὲ τοῦ θεοῦ σημῆναι σαφέστερον ὁπότερα λέγοι. 47, 66 (23, p. 462) ὁ Σωτὴρ σημαίνει ... 48, 15 (24, p. 469) (ὁ θεὸς) κατεῖχεν ἐν τῇ Φωκαίᾳ, θαυμαστὰ οἷα σημαίνων. Cf. ibid. 25 (p. 471). 49, 29 (25, p. 495) τοῦ θεοῦ σημήναντος χρῆσθαι κτλ. (the same ibid. 44 (p. 499)). 51, 1 (27, p. 534) ὁ θεὸς σημαίνει ἔξοδον ἐν Σμύρνῃ ὄντι. Also 52, 1 (28, p. 551).

Apoc. I 4 (ὁ ὢν καὶ ὁ ἦν καὶ ὁ ἐρχόμενος, I 8, IV 8; cf. XI 17, XVI 5): Ael. Arist. 37, 8 (2, p. 15) ἐστί τε καὶ γεγένηται καὶ γενήσεται, sc. Athena.

Apoc. I 17 (ἐγώ εἰμι ὁ πρῶτος καὶ ὁ ἔσχατος, II 8, XXII 13): Ael. Arist. 43, 8 (1, p. 3) οὐδ' ἔστι πρεσβύτερον οὐδὲν Διός. ... ὅδε εστὶ πρῶτος.

Apoc. II 10 (τὸν στέφανον τῆς ζωῆς, passim in Apoc.): Ael. Arist. 27, 36 (16, p. 397) οὗτοι τῷ τῶν ἀθανάτων στεφάνῳ κεκόσμηνται.

Apoc. II 17 (τῷ νικῶντι ... δώσω ... ὄνομα καινόν): Ael. Arist. 8, 11 (32, p. 604) ἐν τοῖς ἄθλοις οἱ νικήσαντες φέρονται τοὔνομα.

Apoc. III 5 (οὐ μὴ ἐξαλείψω τὸ ὄνομα αὐτοῦ): Ael. Arist. 11, 67 (33, p. 640) ἂν μέν τις τοὔνομα τὸ Λακεδαιμονίων ἐξαλείψῃ τοῦ τροπαίου (cf. ibid. 66 (p. 639)).

Apoc. V 2 (τίς ἄξιος ..., vv. 4, 9, 12): Ael. Arist. 1, 51 (13, p. 175) Athens εἶδεν τίνων ἦν ἄξιος (sc. Heracles). Cf. ibid. 54 (p. 176) Athens τῶν ... ὑπηργμένων ἀξίους (sc. the sons of Heracles) εὗρεν.

Apoc. V 3 (ὑποκάτω τῆς γῆς, v. 13; cf. Phil. II 10): Ael. Arist. 40, 8 (5, p. 56) οὐδὲ τῶν κάτω γῆς ἄρα ἠμέλησεν. 46, 8 (3, p. 32) τὸν ὑπὸ γῆς τόπον. 43, 24 (1, p. 9) ὑπὲρ γῆς τε καὶ ὑπὸ γῆν. Cf. 49, 48 (25, p. 500).

Apoc. V 11 (μυριάδες μυριάδων, IX 16): Ael. Arist. 32, 16 (12, p. 139) μυρία δὲ εὐεργετήσας μυρίους οὐδένα πώποτε τῆς εὐεργεσίας μισθὸν ᾔτησεν. ibid. 40 (p. 148) μυρία ... ἐπὶ μυρίοις.

Apoc. VII 9 (ὄχλος πολύς ... περιβεβλημένους στολὰς λευκάς, cf. III 4-5, 18, IV 4, 24, VI 11, VII 13-4, XIX 14; Mt. XVII 2 parr.): Ael. Arist. 48, 30 (24, p. 473) πλῆθος ἀνθρώπων εἶναι λευχειμονούντων καὶ συνεληλυθότων κατὰ τὸν θεόν.

Apoc. VIII 9 (τὰ ἔχοντα ψυχάς = animals): Ael. Arist. 43, 7 (1, p. 2) ὅσα ψυχὴν ἔχει (animals).

Apoc. X 5 (ὁ ἄγγελος ... ἦρεν τὴν χεῖρα αὐτοῦ): Ael. Arist. 45, 33 (8, p. 97) Sarapis χεῖρα ἀντάρας ...

Apoc. XI 7 (τὸ θηρίον τὸ ἀναβαῖνον ἐκ τῆς ἀβύσσου ποιήσει μετ' αὐτῶν πόλεμον, cf. XVII 8): Ael. Arist. 9, 34 (38, p. 724) ἀνὴρ ὑβριστὴς ἐκ τοῦ βαράθρου τῆς γῆς ὁρμώμενος κακῇ μοίρᾳ τῶν Ἑλλήνων, μᾶλλον δ' αὐτοῦ τραφείς, κωμάζει συχνὸν ἤδη χρόνον οὐ φορητά.

Apoc. XI 18 (διαφθεῖραι τοὺς διαφθείροντας τὴν γῆν): Ael. Arist. 40, 4 (5, p. 54) (about Heracles) λῃστὰς δὲ χερσαίους τε καὶ θαλαττίους καὶ πάντας, ὅσοι ῥώμῃ σώματος θαρροῦντες ὕβριζον εἰς τοὺς ἐλάττους, πανωλεθρίᾳ διαφθείρων.

Apoc. XII 9 (the annihilation of the dragon): Ael. Arist. 37, 9 (2, p. 16) πρὸς οὖν τοὺς ἐκείνων [or ἐκείνοις] ὄφεις [συμφύτους] καὶ τἄλλα ὅσα τῆς γῆς ἐφείλκοντο τὸν αὐτῇ σύμφυτον κόσμον καὶ τὸ παρ' αὐτῆς ἀντεπήγαγε (sc. Athena) πῦρ, ἕως ἐξέκαυσεν καὶ ἐξεῖλεν τὸ γένος. For annihilation by fire cf. Apoc. XIV 10, XIX 20, XX 10; Hebr. XII 29.

Apoc. XIII 16 (τοὺς μικροὺς καὶ τοὺς μεγάλους, καὶ τοὺς πλουσίους καὶ τοὺς πτωχούς, καὶ τοὺς ἐλευθέρους καὶ τοὺς δούλους): Ael. Arist. 45, 18 (8, p. 89) ὁμοίως μὲν βασιλεῦσιν, ὁμοίως δὲ ἰδιώταις τίμιος, ὁμοίως δὲ σοφοῖς καὶ φαύλοις, καὶ μεγάλοις καὶ ἐλάττοσι, καὶ καλῶς καὶ τοὐναντίον πράττουσιν. Cf. 26, 66 (14, p. 348).

Apoc. XV 3 (θαυμαστὰ τὰ ἔργα σου, κύριε ὁ θεός): Ael. Arist. 50, 17 (26, p. 506) ἔργον τοῦ θεοῦ θαυμαστόν.

Apoc. XV 3 (ᾄδουσιν...· θαυμαστὰ τὰ ἔργα σου): Ael. Arist. 37, 9 (2, p. 16) τόδε μὲν τὸ ἔργον αὐτῆς (sc. Athena) ... ᾄδεται.

Apoc. XVII 13 and 17 (μία γνώμη): Ael. Arist. 3, 242 (46, p. 253) ὁ μὲν γὰρ ἐφ' ἑαυτῶν τοὺς Λακεδαιμονίους ὁμονοεῖν ἐποίησεν, ὁ δ' Ἀθηναίους καὶ Λακεδαιμονίους τότε ταὐτὸν ἔπεισε φρονῆσαι, μᾶλλον δ' ἅπαντας τοὺς Ἕλληνας μιᾶς γενέσθαι γνώμης. Cf. ibid. 160 (p. 219).

12, 47 (34, p. 660) ἀδίκημα κοινὸν ποιήσονται καὶ μιᾷ γνώμῃ πάντες ὡς ἡμᾶς μεταστήσονται. 23, 31 (42, p. 778) χρὴ δ' ὥσπερ οἰκίαν ἄριστα κατεσκευάσθαι κρίνομεν οὐχ ἥτις ἂν ὡς κάλλιστα λίθων ἔχῃ, ἀλλ' ἥτις ἂν μιᾷ γνώμῃ μάλιστα οἰκῆται, οὕτω καὶ πόλεις ἄριστα νομίζειν οἰκεῖν αἵτινες ἂν ταὐτὸν φρονεῖν ἐπίστωνται. 23, 34 (42, p. 779) ... ὡς ἐκεῖνό γε ἀμήχανον, στρατηγῶν στασιαζόντων καὶ τεταραγμένων πρὸς ἀλλήλους στράτευμα μιᾶς γνώμης γενέσθαι. 23, 42 (42, p. 782) ἐκεῖνοι (sc. Athenians and Spartans) γὰρ μέχρι μὲν ταὐτὰ ἐφρόνουν καὶ μίαν γνώμην εἶχον. 23, 76 (42, p. 794) τὸν πάντα οὐρανὸν καὶ κόσμον ... μία δή που γνώμη καὶ φιλίας δύναμις διοικεῖ. 23, 77 (42, p. 794) πάντων συγκεχωρηκότων καὶ μιᾷ γνώμῃ περὶ παντὸς τοῦ προσήκοντος χρωμένων. 27, 30 (16, p. 394) (M. Antoninus and L. Verus are co-emperors) καὶ οὐδέν γε μᾶλλον τὸ τῆς μοναρχίας ἀγαθὸν διέφθαρται, ἀλλ' ἔστιν μοναρχία θαυμαστὴ δυοῖν σώμασιν καὶ δυοῖν ψυχαῖν μιᾶς γνώμης ἐνιδρυμένης, ὥσπερ τινὸς ἁρμονίας διὰ πασῶν τῶν χορδῶν διηκούσης. 38, 18 (7, p. 77) οὔτε ... ἠλάθησαν οὔθ' ἱκέτευσαν εἰς πόλιν οὐδεμίαν, ἀλλὰ διεξῆλθον καθαροὶ συμφορῶν, μιᾷ φρατρίᾳ καὶ μιᾷ γνώμῃ καὶ τύχῃ χρησάμενοι διὰ τέλους. Cf. further 24, 6.14.25.37 (44, pp. 826, 829, 832, 836). See the collection of texts from other authors in W. C. van Unnik, ΜΙΑ ΓΝΩΜΗ, in: *Studies in John presented to J. N. Sevenster*, Leiden 1970, 209-220.

Apoc. XVIII 8 (ἰσχυρός said of God): Ael. Arist. 43, 16 (1, p. 6) Eros and Ananke are ἰσχυροτάτω.

Apoc. XVIII 11-19 (Babylon's (= Rome's) riches): Ael. Arist. 26, 11-13 (14, p. 326-7) is an elaborate description of Rome's fabulous riches, imported from all over the world.

Apoc. XXI 4 (ὁ θάνατος οὐκ ἔσται ἔτι): Ael. Arist. 43, 14 (1, p. 5) οὐδὲ γῆρας εἴσεισιν εἰς αὐτό, sc. heaven.

Apoc. XXI 6 and XXII 13 (ἐγὼ ... ἡ ἀρχὴ καὶ τὸ τέλος): Ael. Arist. 43, 30-31 (1, p. 11) οὗτος (sc. Ζεὺς) ἁπάντων ἀρχὰς καὶ πέρατα καὶ μέτρα καὶ καιροὺς ἔχων, ἴσον πανταχοῦ πάντων κρατῶν. ... ἀπὸ τούτου ἄρχεσθαι χρὴ καὶ τελευτᾶν εἰς τοῦτον. 45, 22 (8, p. 91) Sarapis ὥσπερ κορυφαῖος πάντων ἀρχὰς καὶ πέρατα ἔχει. See W. C. van Unnik, *Het Godspredicaat 'het begin en het einde' in Flavius Josephus en in de Apocalyps van Johannes* (MKNAW, Afd. Lett., N.R. 39, 1) Amsterdam 1976; on Aristides pp. 52f.

Apoc. XXII 18-19: Ael. Arist. 2, 5 (45, p. 2) καὶ τοῖς μὲν ὅρκοις τοῖς κοινοῖς προσπαραγράφειν ἐξεῖναι ἀνελεῖν καὶ προσθεῖναι ὅ τι ἂν σκοπουμένοις ὕστερον συνδοκῇ. 30, 20 (10, p. 121) (after a quotation from Plato's *Leges* 643c) ... τοῦτ' εἰ δεῖ φῆσαι καλῶς ἔχειν τῷ Πλάτωνι—καὶ γάρ πως ἔτυχον αὐτῶν ἀπομνημονεύσας οὔτ' ἀφελὼν οὐδὲν οὔτε προσθείς—τίς ... See W. C. van Unnik, De la règle μήτε προσθεῖναι μήτε ἀφελεῖν dans l'histoire du canon, *Vigiliae Christianae* 3 (1949), 1-36.

APPENDIX

The passage Ael. Arist. 3, 663-672 (46, pp. 397-404) has long been supposed to be directed against the Christians, because Aristides' opponents are compared to οἱ ἐν τῇ Παλαιστίνῃ δυσσεβεῖς in 671. However, since J. Bernays, *Lukian und die Kyniker*, Berlin 1879, 100ff., it has generally been assumed that Aristides directs himself here against the Cynics (see also E. Norden in *Jahrbücher für classische Philologie*, Suppl. 19, 1893, 404-410, and P. de Labriolle, *La réaction païenne*, Paris 1950[10], 79-87). But because this matter has not yet been fully settled, we quote here some lines which might perhaps aim at the Christians.

(664) ὀνειδίζουσι δὲ τοῖς ἄλλοις, οὐ τῶν πραγμάτων κατεγνωκότες, ἀλλὰ φθονοῦντες ὅτι αὐτοὶ ταῦτα πράττειν οὐ δύνανται (ταῦτα refers to the art of rhetoric). ... (666) ἀλλὰ μὴν τήν γ' ἀπιστίαν καὶ πλεονεξίαν αὐτῶν οὐδὲν δεῖ γνῶναι παρακαταθέμενον, αὐτοὶ γὰρ λαμβάνουσιν ὅ τι ἂν δυνηθῶσιν· οἱ τῷ μὲν ἀποστερεῖν κοινωνεῖν ὄνομα τέθεινται, τῷ δὲ φθονεῖν φιλοσοφεῖν, τῷ δ' ἀπορεῖν ὑπερορᾶν χρημάτων (cf. Acts II 42ff.). ἐπαγγελλόμενοι δὲ φιλανθρωπίαν ὤνησαν μὲν οὐδένα πώποτε, ἐπηρεάζουσι δὲ τοῖς χρωμένοις. ... (668) ..., ἓν τοῦτο σύμβολον κεκτημένοι τοῦ μὴ πρὸς χάριν τοῖς ἀνθρώποις ὁμιλεῖν. ... (671) μόνους δὲ τούτους οὔτ' ἐν κόλαξιν οὔτ' ἐν ἐλευθέροις ἄξιον θεῖναι. ἐξαπατῶσι μὲν γὰρ ὡς κόλακες, προπηλακίζουσι δ' ὡς κρείττονες, δύο τοῖς ἐσχάτοις καὶ τοῖς ἐναντιωτάτοις ἔνοχοι κακοῖς ὄντες, ταπεινότητι καὶ αὐθαδείᾳ, τοῖς ἐν τῇ Παλαιστίνῃ δυσσεβέσι παραπλήσιοι τοὺς τρόπους. καὶ γὰρ ἐκείνοις τοῦτ' ἐστὶ σύμβολον τῆς δυσσεβείας, ὅτι τοὺς κρείττους οὐ νομίζουσι, καὶ οὗτοι τρόπον τινὰ ἀφεστᾶσι τῶν Ἑλλήνων, μᾶλλον δὲ καὶ πάντων τῶν κρειττόνων (all this may refer to the Jews). ... (672) οἱ λόγον μὲν ἔγκαρπον οὐδένα πώποτ' οὔτ' εἶπον οὔθ' εὗρον οὔτ' ἐποίησαν, οὐ πανηγύρεις ἐκόσμησαν, οὐ θεοὺς ἐτίμησαν, οὐ πόλεσι συνεβούλευσαν, οὐ λυπουμένους παρεμυθήσαντο, οὐ στασιάζοντας διήλλαξαν, οὐ προύτρεψαν νέους, οὐκ ἄλλους οὐδένας, οὐ κόσμου τοῖς λόγοις προὐνοήσαντο.

BIBLIOGRAPHY OF WORKS ON AELIUS ARISTIDES

EDITIONS

Dindorf, W., *Aristides*, 3 vols., Leipzig 1829 (repr. Hildesheim 1964); (contains all orations and the scholia).

Keil, B., *Aelii Aristidis quae supersunt omnia*, vol. II, Berlin 1898 (repr. Berlin 1958; vol. I was never published); (contains orations 17-53).

Schmid, W., *Aristidis quae feruntur Libri Rhetorici II*, Leipzig 1926 (contains the *Ars Rhetorica*).

Behr, C. A., *Aristides*, vol. I (Loeb Classical Library), Cambridge (Mass.)—London 1973 (contains orations 1 and 2).

Lenz, F. W.,—Behr, C. A., *P. Aelii Aristidis opera quae exstant omnia*, vol. I, Leiden 1976— . . . (contains orations 1-8 so far).

STUDIES

(The only books and articles that have been listed here are those published since Baumgart's classic study of 1874)

Amann, J., *Die Zeusrede des Ailios Aristeides* (Tübinger Beiträge zur Altertumswissenschaft 12), Tübingen 1931.

Baumgart, H., *Aelius Aristides als Repräsentant der sophistischen Rhetorik des zweiten Jahrhunderts der Kaiserzeit*, Leipzig 1874.

Beecke, E., *Die historischen Angaben in Aelius Aristides' Panathenaikos auf ihre Quellen untersucht*, diss. Strassburg 1905.

Behr, C. A., *Aelius Aristides and the Sacred Tales*, Amsterdam 1968.

Behr, C. A., Citations of Porphyry's 'Against Aristides' Preserved in Olympiodorus, *American Journal of Philology* 89 (1968), 186-199.

Behr, C. A., Aelius Aristides' Birth Date Corrected to November 26, 117 A.D., *American Journal of Philology* 90 (1969), 75-79.

Behr, C. A., Aelius Aristides and the Egyptian Gods, in *Hommages à Maarten J. Vermaseren* I, Leiden 1978, 13-24.

Bengtson, H., Das Imperium Romanum in griechischer Sicht, *Gymnasium* 71 (1964), 150-166.

Bernays, J., Die Reden des Aristides gegen Platon; ein Beitrag zur Literaturgeschichte, in: idem, *Gesammelte Abhandlungen* II, Berlin 1885, 362-364.

Björck, G., Ὄναρ ἰδεῖν: de la perception de la rêve chez les anciens *Eranos* 44 (1946), 306-314.

Bleicken, J., Der Preis des Aelius Aristides auf das römische Weltreich, *Nachrichten der Akad. der Wiss. in Göttingen, Phil.-hist. Klasse,* Göttingen 1966.

Bonner, C., Some Phases of Religious Feeling in Later Paganism, *Harvard Theological Review* 30 (1937), 119-140.

Boulanger, A., Chronologie de la vie du rhéteur Aelius Aristide, *Revue de Philologie* 46 (1922), 26-54.

Boulanger, A., Lucien et Aelius Aristide, *Revue de Philologie* 47 (1923), 144-151.

Boulanger, A., *Aelius Aristide et la sophistique dans la province d'Asie au IIe siècle de notre ère,* Paris 1923 (repr. Paris 1968).

Bowersock, G., *Greek Sophists in the Roman Empire,* Oxford 1969.

Bowersock, G., Greek Intellectuals and the Imperial Cult in the Second Century A.D., in: W. den Boer *et al., Le culte des souverains dans l'empire romain* (Entretiens sur l'antiquité classique XIX), Vandœuvres- Geneva 1973, 177-212.

Büchner, W., Zu Aelius Aristides, *Philologus* 49 (1890), 182-183.

Christ, W., - Schmid, W., - Stählin, O., *Geschichte der griechischen Literatur* II 2, München 1924.

Dill, S., *Roman Society from Nero to Marcus Aurelius,* New York 1960 [4].

Dodds, E. R., *The Greeks and the Irrational,* Berkeley 1951.

Dodds, E. R., *Pagans and Christians in an Age of Anxiety,* Cambridge 1965.

Dodds, E. R., Supernormal Phenomena in Classical Antiquity, *Proceedings of the Society for Psychical Research* 55, part 203 (1971), 189-237.

Dölger, F. J., Der Heiland, in: idem, *Antike und Christentum* VI, Münster 1950, 241-272.

Domaszewski, A. von, Beiträge zur Kaisergeschichte II: Die Rede des Aristides εἰς βασιλέα, *Philologus* 65 (1906), 344-356.

Edelstein, E. and L., *Asclepius,* 2 vols., Baltimore 1945.

Egle, F., *Untersuchungen über die Echtheit der Rede* Ἀπελλᾶ γενεθλιακός *des Ailios Aristeides,* diss. Tübingen 1906.

Erhard, H., Arzt und Priester in Pergamon, *Gesnerus* 11 (1954), 11-16.

Festugière, A.-J., *Personal Religion Among the Greeks,* Berkeley 1954.

Festugière, A.-J., Sur les "Discours Sacrés" d'Aelius Aristide, *Revue des Études Grecques* 82 (1969), 117-153.

Früchtel, L., Aristides Rhetor, *Reallexikon für Antike und Christentum* I (1950), 654-656.
Gärtner, H., Aristeides (3), *Der Kleine Pauly* I (1964), 557-559.
Gerth, K., Zweite Sophistik, *PW (RE) Suppl.* VIII (1956), 719-782.
Gigli, D., Teoria e prassi metrica negli inni A Sarapide e Dioniso di Elio Aristide, *Prometheus* 1 (1975), 237-265.
Giuliano, A., Aristide di Smirne, *Dialoghi di Archeologia* 1 (1967), 72-81.
Gourevitch, M. and D., Le cas Aelius Aristide ou mémoires d'un hystérique au IIe siècle, *Informations psychiatriques* 44 (1968), 897-902.
Groag, E., Die Kaiserrede des Pseudo-Aristides, *Wiener Studien* 40 (1918), 20-45.
Groningen, B. A. van, Literary Tendencies in the Second Century A.D., *Mnemosyne* IV 18 (1965), 42-56.
Haas, A., *Quibus fontibus Aelius Aristides in componenda declamatione quae inscribitur* Πρὸς Πλάτωνα ὑπὲρ τῶν τεττάρων *usus sit*, diss. Greifswald 1884.
Harry, J. E., On the Authorship of the Leptinean Orations Attributed to Aristides, *American Journal of Philology* 15 (1894), 66-73.
Henrichs, A., - Browne, G., A Papyrus of Aristides' Panathenaikos (P. Mich. inv. 6651), *Zeitschrift für Papyrologie und Epigraphik* 2 (1968), 171-175.
Herzog, R., Ein Asklepios-Hymnus des Aristeides von Smyrna, *Sitzungsberichte der preussischen Akad. der Wissenschaften, Phil.-hist. Klasse* 23, Berlin 1934, 753-770.
Höfler, A., *Der Sarapishymnus des Aelios Aristeides* (Tübinger Beiträge zur Altertumswissenschaft 27), Tübingen 1935.
Hubbel, H. M., *The Influence of Isocrates on Cicero, Dionysius and Aristides*, diss. Yale, New Haven 1913.
Hug, A., *Leben und Werke des Rhetors Aristides*, diss. Freiburg 1912.
Jones, C. P., Aelius Aristides εἰς Ῥώμην 43K, *American Journal of Philology* 85 (1964), 65.
Jones, C. P., Aelius Aristides, εἰς βασιλέα, *Journal of Roman Studies* 62 (1972), 134-152.
Keil, B., Eine Kaiserrede, *Nachrichten der königlichen Gesellschaft der Wissenschaften zu Göttingen, Phil.-hist. Klasse*, Göttingen 1905, 381-428.
Keil, B., Die pseudo-aristideischen Leptineen, *Hermes* 71 (1936), 171-185.

Kennedy, G., *The Art of Persuasion in Greece*, London 1963.
Kennedy, G., *The Art of Rhetoric in the Roman World*, Princeton 1972.
Kessels, A. H. M., Review of C. A. Behr, *Aelius Aristides and the Sacred Tales* (1968), *Mnemosyne* IV 24 (1971), 102-104.
Kienast, T., Die Homonoiaverträge in der römischen Kaiserzeit, *Jahrbuch für Numismatik und Geldgeschichte* 14 (1964), 51-64.
Kindstrand, J. F., *Homer in der zweiten Sophistik. Studien zu der Homerlektüre und dem Homerbild bei Dion von Prusa, Maximos von Tyros und Aelios Aristides* (Acta Univ. Upsal.: Studia Graeca Upsal. VII), Stockholm 1973.
Knox, W. L., *Some Hellenistic Elements in Primitive Christianity*, Cambridge 1943.
Labriolle, P. de, *La réaction païenne*, Paris 1934.
Leeuw, C. A. de, *Aelius Aristides als bron voor de kennis van zijn tijd*, diss. Utrecht 1939, Amsterdam 1939.
Lenz, F. W., *The Aristides Prolegomena* (Supplements to Mnemosyne 5), Leiden 1959.
Lenz, F. W., *Fünf Reden Thomas Magisters*, Leiden 1963.
Lenz, F. W., Der Athenahymnus des Aristeides, *Rivista di cultura classica e medioevale* 5 (1963), 329-347.
Lenz, F. W., *Aristeidesstudien*, Berlin 1964.
Lenz, F. W., Zum Text des Πρεσβευτικὸς πρὸς 'Αχιλλέα des Aristeides, *Philologus* 109 (1965), 146-151.
Lenz, F. W., Aristidea et epigrammatica, *Wiener Studien* N.F. 2 (1968), 28-45.
Lenz, F. W., Zwei Misshandlungen des Perikles und des Areopags im Aristeidestext, *Philologus* 112 (1968), 276-281.
Lenz, F. W., Zu den neuen Aristeidespapyri, *Philologus* 113 (1969), 301-306.
Lenz, F. W., Review of C. A. Behr, *Aelius Aristides and the Sacred Tales* (1968), *Gnomon* 42 (1970), 244-250.
Levin, S., *Aristides, To Rome, Translated with Notes and Introduction*, Glencoe 1950.
Lind, L. R., Concept, Action, and Character: The Reason for Rome's Greatness, *Transactions and Proceedings of the American Philological Association* 103 (1972), 235-283.
Meier, C. A., *Antike Inkubation und Moderne Psychotherapie*, Zürich 1949.
Meier, C. A., Le rêve et l'incubation dans l'ancienne Grèce, in: *Le rêve et les sociétés humaines*, Paris 1967, 290-305.

Mensching, E., Zu Aelius Aristides' 33. Rede, *Mnemosyne* IV 18 (1965), 57-63.

Mesk, J., Zu den Prosa- und Vershymnen des Aelius Aristides, *Raccolta di scritti in onore di Felice Ramorino*, Milano 1927, 660-672.

Mesk, J., *Der Aufbau der XXVI. Rede des Aelius Aristides* (35. Jahresbericht des Franz-Joseph-Realgymnasiums), Wien 1909.

Michel, A., De Socrate à Maxime de Tyre; les problèmes de l'armée dans l'idéologie romaine, *Revue des Études Latines* 47 (1969), 237-251.

Michenaud, G., - Dierkens, J., *Les rêves dans les "Discours sacrés" d'Aelius Aristide, IIe siècle ap. J.-C.; Essai d'analyse psychologique*, Mons 1972.

Misch, G., *Geschichte der Autobiographie* I, Bern 1944[3].

Nilsson, M. P., *Geschichte der griechischen Religion* II, München 1961 [2].

Nock, A. D., *Conversion*, Oxford 1933.

Norden, E., Beiträge zur Geschichte der griechischen Philosophie, *Jahrbücher für classische Philologie, Supplementband* 19 (1893), 404-410.

Norden, E., *Die antike Kunstprosa*, 2 vols., Leipzig 1915-1918[3].

Oliver, J. H., *The Ruling Power. A Study of the Roman Empire in the Second Century after Christ through the Roman Oration of Aelius Aristides* (Transactions of the American Philosophical Society 43:4), Philadelphia 1953.

Oliver, J. H., *The Civilizing Power. A Study of the Panathenaic Discourse of Aelius Aristides against the Background of Literature and Cultural Conflict* (Transactions of the American Philosophical Society 58:1), Philadelphia 1968.

Oliver, J. H., Aristides, In Romam 65, No Parallel for P. Giessen 40, *La Parola del Passato* 23 (1968), 50-52.

Pack, R., Two Sophists and Two Emperors, *Classical Philology* 42 (1947), 17-20.

Pavan, M., Sul significato storico dell' Encomio di Roma di Elio Aristide, *Parola del Passato* 17 (1962), 81-95.

Phillips, E. D., A Hypochondriac and his God, *Greece and Rome* 21 (1952), 23-36.

Phillips, E. D., Three Greek Writers on the Roman Empire, *Classica et Mediaevalia* 18 (1957), 102-119.

Ratti, E., Imperio romano e armonia dell' universo nella pratica retorica e nella concezione religiosa di Elio Aristide; Una ricerca per l' Εἰς Ῥώμην, *Mem. di Ist. Lombardo, Cl. di Lett., Scr. mor. e stor.* XXXI 4, Milano 1971, 283-361.

Real, C. A. del, *Noticias sobre España en Elio Aristides de Esmirna*, Madrid 1950.

Reardon, B. P., *Courants littéraires grecs des 2e et 3e siècles après Jésus Christ*, Paris 1971.

Reardon, B. P., The Anxious Pagan, *Echos du Monde Classique* 17 (1973), 81-93.

Rengstorf, K. H., *Die Anfänge der Auseinandersetzung zwischen Christusglaube und Asklepiosfrömmigkeit*, Münster 1953.

Richtsteig, F., Bericht über die Literatur zu Aristeides aus den Jahren 1926-1930, *Jahresbericht über die Fortschritte der klassischen Altertumswissenschaft* 238 (1931), 15-22.

Romilly, J. de, *Magic and Rhetoric in Ancient Greece*, Cambridge (Mass.)-London 1975.

Roulet, F. C., L'Asklépieion de Pergame, *Gesnerus* 9 (1952), 1-8.

Schmid, W., *Der Atticismus in seinen Hauptvertretern*, 4 vols., Stuttgart 1887-1896 (repr. Hildesheim 1964).

Schmid, W., Die Lebensgeschichte des Rhetors Aristides, *Rheinisches Museum* 48 (1893), 53-83.

Schmid, W., Eine Reise des Aelius Aristides in die Milyas, *Rheinisches Museum* 50 (1895), 308-310.

Schmid, W., Aristeides, *PW (RE)* II (1896), 886-894.

Schmid, W., Das Geburtsjahr des Aelius Aristides, *Philologus* 56 (1897), 721-2.

Schmid, W., Die sogenannte Aristeidesrhetorik, *Rheinisches Museum* 72 (1917/18), 113-149; 238-257.

Schmid, W., Review of A. Boulanger, *Aelius Aristide* ... (1923), *Philologische Wochenschrift* 44 (1924), 1-14.

Schwabl, H., Zeus (Teil II), *PW Suppl.* XV (1978), 1372-79.

Sieveking, W., *De Aelii Aristidis oratione* εἰς Ῥώμην, diss. Göttingen 1919.

Sohlberg, D., Aelius Aristides und Diogenes von Babylon, Zur Geschichte des rednerischen Ideals, *Museum Helveticum* 29 (1972), 177-200; 256-277.

Stella, L. A., Εἰς Ῥώμην. *In gloria di Roma; Orazione di Elio Aristide; Introduzione, traduzione e commentario*, Rome 1940.

Swift, L. J., The Anonymous Encomium of Philip the Arab, *Greek, Roman, and Byzantine Studies* 7 (1966), 267-289.

Szelest, H., De Aelii Aristidis clausulis rhythmicis in orationibus quae Μέλεται atque Μαντευταὶ inscribuntur obviis, *Eos* 50 (1959/60), 91-98.

Turzewitsch, I., Zur Zeusrede, *Philologische Wochenschrift* 52 (1932), 222-3.

Uerschels, W., *Der Dionysoshymnos des Aelius Aristides*, diss. Bonn 1962.

Vittinghof, F., Review of J. H. Oliver, *The Ruling Power* (1953), *Gnomon* 29 (1957), 74-76.

Voll, W., *Der Dionysoshymnos des Aelius Aristides*, diss. Tübingen 1948 (unpubl.).

Waddell, W. G., On Egypt. A Discourse by P. Aelius Aristides of Smyrna, *Bulletin of the Faculty of Arts of the University of Egypt* II 2 (1934), 121-166.

Wahl, W., *Der Herakleshymnos des Aelius Aristides*, diss. Tübingen 1946 (unpubl.).

Weinreich, O., *Antike Heilungswunder* (RGVV VIII 1), Giessen 1909.

Weinreich, O., Typisches und Individuelles in der Religiosität des Aelios Aristeides, in: idem, *Ausgewählte Schriften* I, Amsterdam 1969, 298-310.

Weinreich, O., Hymnologica, *ibid.* 311-318.

Weinreich, O., Neue Urkunden zur Sarapisreligion, *ibid.* 410-442.

Welcker, F. G., Inkubation: Aristides der Rhetor, in: idem, *Kleine Schriften* III, Bonn 1950, 89-157.

Wendland, P., *Die hellenistisch-römische Kultur in ihren Beziehungen zu Judentum und Christentum*, Tübingen 1912 [2-3].

Wikenhauser, A., Doppelträume, *Biblica* 29 (1948), 100-111.

Wilamowitz-Moellendorff, U. von, Review of A. Boulanger, *Aelius Aristide* . . . (1923), *Litteris* 2 (1925), 125-130.

Wilamowitz-Moellendorff, U., von, Der Rhetor Aristides, *Sitzungsber. der preussischen Akad. der Wiss., Phil.-hist. Klasse* 28, Berlin 1925, 333-353.

Wright, W. C., Review of A. Boulanger, *Aelius Aristide*. . . (1923), *Classical Philology* 18 (1923), 355-358.

Zucker, F., Zosimos, Erzieher des Rhetors Aristeides, *PW(RE)* X A (1972), 787-790.

THE INDEXES

The first index enables the reader to see which passages from Aelius Aristides have been mentioned, and where they can be found. For the order of the works, the new critical edition of Behr (see Introd.) and Keil's edition of 1898 have been followed. Though the orations 25 and 35 Keil, 53 and 54 Dind., and the Ars Rhetorica are generally held to be spurious, a few parallels from them have nevertheless been adopted.

The second index has been compiled because passages from Aelius Aristides can often be compared with several N.T. passages at the same time. They have been regularly quoted here in the first N.T. context where it seemed useful to do so, or in connexion with the most strikingly parallel passage in the N.T. In these cases, the other N.T. passages with which a given parallel from Aelius Aristides could be compared, are referred to in brackets. The second index enables the reader to find the N.T. passages referred to between brackets. For example, to find the parallel to Acts I 1 the reader is referred to Luke I 3.

The third index is a select index of subjects.

INDEX OF QUOTATIONS FROM AELIUS ARISTIDES

Ael. Arist.	N.T.
1,298	Lk. I 66
1,299	2 Tim. I 10-11
1,301	Mt. V 22
	Rom. III 5
1,313	Rom. I 23
	Rom. XV 28
1,315	1 Thess. II 7
1,317	Hebr. XI 32
1,321	Acts V 29
1,324	Acts XXI 37b
1,326	Acts V 29
	Acts XXI 37b
1,329	Gal. III 8
1,330	Rom. II 19f.
	1 Cor. I 22
1,335	Rom. III 4
1,338	Rom. X 2
	2 Ptr. I 17
1,341	2 Cor. XII 1-4
1,349	Hebr. VIII 1
1,354	Acts XVII 16
	Acts XIX 35
1,355	Lk. V 36-39
1,360	Mt. I 1
1,364	Acts XVII 16
1,366	1 Cor. XI 23
1,367	Acts XVII 19
1,368	Acts XXII 3
1,374	Acts I 1ff.
1,375	Hebr. VII 9
1,382	Jas. IV 12
1,385	Acts XVII 19
1,390	Rom. II 14
	Jas. II 1-9
1,397	1 Cor. II 1
1,399	1 Cor. IX 25
1,402	1 Cor. IX 24
1,404	Acts VII 10

2 Πρὸς Πλάτωνα ὑπὲρ ῥητορικῆς

Ael. Arist.	N.T.
2,1	1 Tim. V 13
2,5	Apoc. XXII 18-19
2,19	Acts XIV 12
2,29	Tit. I 13
2,33	Rom. I 8
2,34-43	1 Cor. XII + XIV
2,34	Acts V 29
2,39	Acts XV 28
2,40	Acts I 8
	Hebr. VII 9
2,47	Acts XVI 16
2,49	Acts VIII 36
2,53	Acts II 4
	Acts V 29
2,67	Mk. V 25-29
2,68	Rom. I 14
2,69	Hebr. VI 18
2,71	Mt. II 13
2,76	Phil. IV 3
2,93	1 Cor. III 18
2,115	Mt. VI 25
2,119	2 Tim. III 14
2,120	1 Cor. XI 14
2,127	Apoc. I 1
2,128	Eph. VI 5ff.
2,129	1 Tim. II 9-14
2,139-140	Mt. XVIII 15
2,148	Acts VIII 36
	Hebr. VII 9
2,169	Acts VII 22
2,192	Acts XVII 30
2,195	Tit. III 3
2,197	Rom. XII 16
	Hebr. VII 9
2,212	1 Tim. I 9
2,214	Mk. IV 11
2,224	Phil. II 7
2,225	Mt. V 25
2,230	Acts XXVI 14
2,254	Rom. III 9
2,258	Jas. V 15
2,261	1 Cor. VI 7-8
2,271	Acts VIII 36
2,279	Lk. XXIV 19
2,293	Rom. III 9
2,297	Acts XVII 30
2,321	1 Cor. XII 4-31
2,323	1 Thess. II 5
	Jude 3
2,324	2 Tim. II 15
2,328	1 Thess. II 5
2,336	Mk. I 44
2,358	Acts VIII 36
2,361	Acts VIII 36
2,387	Mt. XX 28
	1 Tim. V 13
2,389-390	2 Cor. III 16f.
2,391	1 Tim. V 13
2,394	1 Tim. IV 7
2,396	Acts XIV 12
2,410	2 Ptr. I 4
2,412	Acts VIII 36
2,418	1 Cor. IX 25
	1 Cor. XVI 17

Ael. Arist.	N.T.
12,8	Rom. VIII 6
	Gal. VI 12
12,18	Acts VIII 36
12,19	Rom. I 8
12,34	Acts XIV 22
12,35	1 Ptr. II 19
12,41	Rom. IX 19
12,47	Apoc. XVII 13.17
12,49	Hebr. III 13
12,54	Rom. II 1
	1 Cor. IX 25
12,57	Mt. VI 2
13 Λευκτρικός Γ	
13,12	Rom. XII 16
13,16	Phil. II 7-8
13,20	Acts VIII 36
	1 Cor. XIII 13
15 Λευκτρικός Ε	
15,16	Acts IX 1
15,29	Hebr. XI 7
15,40	Hebr. VIII 1
16 Πρεσβευτικὸς πρὸς Ἀχιλλέα	
16,12	Rom. III 9
16,13	Mt. XIX 29
16,31	Rom. I 9
16,35	Acts VIII 36
16,41	Col. III 8-9
17 Σμυρναϊκός	
17,7	Hebr. XI 32
17,9	Rom. XII 4-5
17,18	1 Tim. I 9
18 Ἐπὶ Σμύρνῃ μονῳδία	
18,7	Mt. XXIV 6
19 Ἐπιστολὴ περὶ Σμύρνης πρὸς τοὺς βασιλέας	
19,1	Acts XV 23
20 Παλινῳδία ἐπὶ Σμύρνῃ	
20,1	Rom. XIII 1b
21 Σμυρναϊκός (προσφωνητικός)	
21,3	Mt. I 1
21,5	Rom. XII 4-5
22 Ἐλευσίνιος	
22,3	Acts V 29
	2 Cor. XII 1-4

Ael. Arist.	N.T.
23 Περὶ ὁμονοίας ταῖς πόλεσιν	
23,2	Mk. I 1
23,14	Lk. I 47
23,15	Mt. XXII 14
	John I 9
23,17	Hebr. VI 18-19
23,18	Mt. XXII 29
23,19	John VI 28-29
23,25	John V 23
	Acts XIX 27
23,31	Apoc. XVII 13.17
23,34	Apoc. XVII 13.17
23,42	Apoc. XVII 13.17
23,61	Acts IV 29
23,65	Rom. XII 16
23,69	Mt. VI 25
23,71	Rom. XII 19-21
23,76	1 Ptr. III 3-4
	Apoc. XVII 13.17
23,77	Eph. V 1
	Apoc. XVII 13.17
23,79	Mt. I 20
	Acts XX 28
	Acts XXIV 2
23,80	Rom. III 4
24 Ῥοδίοις περὶ ὁμονοίας	
24,6	Rom. XII 16
	Apoc. XVII 13.17
24,8	Rom. XII 16
24,14	Apoc. XVII 13.17
24,25	Apoc. XVII 13.17
24,26	Jude 3
24,29	Rom. XII 16
24,32	Rom. I 29ff.
24,33	Eph. VI 1-9
24,35	Rom. II 14
24,37	Eph. IV 27
	Apoc. XVII 13.17
24,38	Rom. XII 16
24,39	Rom. XII 4-5
	2 Ptr. II 5
24,42	Acts II 44
	Acts XXII 3
24,44	Jude 13
24,46	John V 39
24,48	John V 23
24,49	Rom. XII 16
24,50	1 Tim. II 8
25 Ῥοδιακός	
25,12	Rom. VII 8

Ael. Arist.	N.T.
40,18	Acts I 8
40,22	Acts III 13
	Acts VII 31
	Rom. VIII 17
41 Διόνυσος	
41,3	Eph. II 14
	2 Ptr. I 17
41,7	Mt. XXII 29
	Lk. XIII 16
	1 John III 8
41,8	Rom. XV 12
41,9	1 Cor. XIV 34ff.
41,10	Acts XIV 17
	Tit. III 4
42 Λαλιὰ εἰς Ἀσκληπιόν	
42,1	Lk. II 29
	Lk. II 37
	2 Cor. VIII 22
42,4	Mt. VII 22
	Lk. I 47
	Acts III 13
	1 Thess. IV 9
42,5	Acts X 38
42,6	Mk. IX 27
42,7	Mt. IV 24
	1 Tim. II 13
42,8	Lk. V 26
42,10	Mt. VIII 26
	Acts IV 30
42,11	Mt. X 19
42,12	Tit. III 4
42,13	Mt. I 20
	Eph. I 6
42,15	Eph. I 16
43	Εἰς Δία
43,1	Mt. I 21
	Mt. V 23f.
	Mt. X 19
	Lk. I 47
	1 Tim. I 17
	1 John II 28
43,2	Lk. I 1
	Acts XII 11
	Acts XVII 31
	2 Cor. XI 26
	Eph. V 19
43,4	Hebr. VII 9
	Hebr. VIII 8
43,5	1 Tim. VI 12

Ael. Arist	N.T.
43,6	Mt. V 16
	John IV 10
	John VI 28-29
	John XVI 30
	Acts II 11
	Eph. IV 6
43,7	Acts XIV 15
	Acts XVII 24a
	Rom. I 20
	Phil. II 10
	Col. I 15-20
	Apoc. VIII 9
43,8	Acts III 15
	Acts XXII 3
	Apoc. I 17
43,8-9	John I 1
43,9	John I 3
	Acts XVII 25
	Rom. XI 36
43,10	2 Tim. I 9
43,11	Eph. III 17
	Hebr. I 10
43,13	John I 3
	Eph. III 20
43,14-15	Hebr. XI 10
43,14	Acts XVII 26a
	Jude 6
	Apoc. XXI 4
43,15	Eph. IV 6
	Hebr. I 6
	Hebr. III 4
	Hebr. XIII 14
43,16	Acts XVII 28b
	2 Ptr. I 4
	Apoc. XVIII 8
43,17	Mt. XII 12
43,18	Mk. I 44
	Acts XVII 30
	Eph. II 2
	Eph. III 10
43,19	Mt. VI 25-32
	Mt. VII 11
	Rom. XV 12
	1 Cor. XIV 33
	2 Thess. I 3
43,20	Mt. XXVI 42
	John IV 34
	Acts XVII 28b
	Hebr. VII 11
43,21	Lk. I 71
43,22	Acts XXVI 16
	Hebr. VI 17
	Jas. I 17b

Ael. Arist.	N.T.
43,23	Acts XVII 24a
	Acts XVII 28a
	Phil. II 10
	Hebr. II 10
	Hebr. V 9
	Hebr. XI 10
43,24-26	Acts XIV 17
43,24	Mt. V 45
	Acts XVII 26b
	Acts XXVII 13-44
	Apoc. V 3
43,25	Lk. VI 19
	Lk. VII 30
	Acts V 29
	Acts X 38
	Acts XIX 23ff.
	Acts XXVIII 11
	Hebr. VI 17
43,26	Acts XVII 27b
	Eph. I 23b
43,27	Hebr. IV 13
43,28	Eph. V 1
43,29	Eph. IV 6
	Col. I 15-20
	1 Ptr. II 25
43,30-31	Apoc. XXI 6
	Apoc. XXII 13
43,30	Mt. V 48
	Lk. I 47
	Lk. V 21
	Acts XIV 17
	1 Cor. XV 57
	Gal. V 1
	Hebr. IV 16
	Hebr. XIII 6
43,31	Mt. X 19
	Hebr. XII 2

44 Εἰς τὸ Αἰγαῖον πέλαγος

Ael. Arist.	N.T.
44,3	Lk. II 1
44,11	Eph. IV 6
44,16	1 Cor. I 26-28

45 Εἰς Σάραπιν

Ael. Arist.	N.T.
45,4	Hebr. VII 9
45,5	John V 23
45,8	Rom. XIII 2
	Gal. III 17
45,14	Mt. X 19
	Mk. X 27
	Hebr. II 10
	Hebr. XIII 6
45,15	Rom. I 19ff.
	Jas. I 17a
45,16	Mt. X 19
	John IV 10
	John VI 28-29
	2 Cor. IX 15
45,17	Acts XVII 28b
45,18	Mt. V 18
	Lk. II 52
	Eph. II 12
	Apoc. XIII 16
45,20	Acts V 29
	Acts VIII 50
	Acts XVII 25
	1 Tim. IV 10
45,21	Eph. I 23b
45,22	Apoc. XXI 6
45,23	Acts XIX 28.34
45,23f.	Mk. XII 29
45,24	Mt. XVI 19
45,25	Rom. II 6
	Rom. XI 33
45,26	Lk. I 50
	Rom. XV 13
	Tit. III 4
	Hebr. X 31
45,27	Mt. XVIII 20
	1 Cor. X 18
45,28	Hebr. VII 2.4.6
45,29	Mt. IV 23
	Mt. VIII 26
45,30	John XXI 25
45,31	John XXI 24
45,32	Mt. VI 26
	Acts XIX 20
	2 Cor. XII 1-4
45,33	John I 4
	Acts XXVII 13-44
	Apoc. X 5

46 Ἰσθμικὸς εἰς Ποσειδῶνα

Ael. Arist.	N.T.
46,2	Acts IX 38
46,3	Lk. XI 13
	Lk. XVIII 13
46,4	Hebr. VIII 12
46,5	Eph. IV 9
46,7	Acts X 43
46,8	Apoc. V 3
46,9	Rom. VI 8
	Gal. I 4
	Eph. II 19
	Tit. III 4

INDEX OF NEW TESTAMENT REFERENCES

OLD TESTAMENT REFERENCES

SELECT INDEX OF SUBJECTS